The Race for the New Frontier
International Competition
in Advanced Technology–
Decisions for America

Panel on Advanced Technology
Competition

Office of International Affairs

National Research Council

A TOUCHSTONE BOOK
A National Academy Press/Simon & Schuster Publication
New York

Part One of this book was previously published by
The National Academy Press under the title *International
Competition in Advanced Technology: Decisions for America*
(Library of Congress Catalog Card Number: 83-60712).

A Touchstone Book
Published by Simon & Schuster, Inc.
Simon & Schuster Building
Rockefeller Center
1230 Avenue of the Americas
New York, New York 10020
TOUCHSTONE and colophon are registered trademarks of
Simon & Schuster, Inc.

Designed by Patricia Girvin Dunbar
Manufactured in the United States of America

1 2 3 4 5 6 7 8 9 10

Library of Congress Cataloging in Publication Data
National Research Council (U.S.). Panel on Advanced
Technology Competition and the Industrialized Allies.

The race for the new frontier.

(A Touchstone book)
Bibliography: p.
Includes index
1. Technology and state—United States. 2. High
technology industries—United States. I. Title.
T21.N34 1984   338.4′76′0973   84-5470
ISBN 0-671-49964-5

Note

The National Research Council was established by the National Academy of Sciences in 1916 to associate the broad community of science and technology with the Academy's purposes of furthering knowledge and of advising the federal government. The Council operates in accordance with general policies determined by the Academy under the authority of its Congressional charter of 1863, which establishes the Academy as a private, nonprofit, self-governing membership corporation. The Council has become the principal operating agency of both the National Academy of Sciences and the National Academy of Engineering in the conduct of their services to the government, the public, and the scientific and engineering communities. It is administered jointly by both Academies and the Institute of Medicine. The National Academy of Engineering and the Institute of Medicine were established in 1964 and 1970, respectively, under the charter of the National Academy of Sciences.

This study was supported by the Executive Office of the President, Office of Science and Technology Policy, and the National Academy of Sciences. The NAS contribution was drawn from funds used for Academy-initiated studies; funds were provided by a consortium of private foundations. Consortium members include the Carnegie Corporation of New York, the Charles E. Culpeper Foundation, the William and Flora Hewlett Foundation, the John D. and Catherine T. MacArthur Foundation, the Andrew W. Mellon Foundation, and the Rockefeller Foundation.

Contents

Foreword

The Race for the New Frontier addresses one of the most important issues facing the United States in recent years. Concerns about declining American industrial productivity, about the education of future scientists and engineers, and about the continuing health of our advanced technology industries have become major topics of debate in Congress and elsewhere throughout the government. This book—which consists of the report issued by a panel of distinguished businessmen, economists, scientists, and former government officials and includes the background papers commissioned by the panel—represents a valuable contribution to the ongoing discussion of these matters.

Such inputs from a broad spectrum of knowledgeable individuals with experience in different aspects of international trade and domestic economic policy are essential if we are to make wise decisions about the future course of America as we become increasingly integrated into the world economy. The relationship of government to industry, of industry to industry, and of industry to universities is coming under closer scrutiny as we attempt to meet the economic challenges posed by rapidly growing industrial economies, such as those of Japan, Western Europe, and the newly industrializing developing countries. Both Congress and the administration face complex questions involving not only international trade policy, but also domestic policies toward taxation, industry regulation, support for research, national educational priorities, and the proper role of government in fostering greater competitiveness.

For example, the Congress in the past three years has significantly increased tax incentives for research and development, and is considering a variety of other proposals to foster innovation. Such measures seek to provide a favorable, government-created climate for private sector development, in addition to furthering the government's more traditional activities of supporting education and basic research. It is important that the government strive to maintain a continuing awareness of the status of our advanced technology industries both at home and in the international marketplace, so that government policy can be coordinated with industry needs.

It is my hope that the managers of advanced technology enterprises will increasingly share in the decision-making process that affects the climate in which they do business. To do that effectively, they need to be aware of the global political and economic forces affecting their businesses as well as specific developments in their industries. Reports such as the one presented here are an important source of such information. This report significantly enriched the understanding of the Committee on Finance of these issues when it was presented to the Committee at a hearing on April 14, 1983. I anticipate that it will make an important contribution to the growing public debate over the next few years, while elevating our national comprehension of the complexity of the issues and its impact on all Americans.

Robert Dole
Chairman
Committee on Finance
United States Senate

Preface

A central new policy concern—international trade and competitiveness in advanced technology—has risen sharply in importance in the United States and in its closest allies and trading partners. Because of the significance of this issue with regard to national security and overall economic strength, leaders in these countries are focusing urgent attention on their nations' capabilities for innovation and competition in advanced technology markets. Discussions of these concerns take place at the highest levels of government, at economic summit meetings, and at other multilateral events, for the effect of high technology on the maufacturing and service sectors is profound.

In the United States alone, the development of innovative capacity and competitiveness in advanced technology will remain high on the list of national priorities for years to come. In all American industries—from textiles to automobiles to metals refining—the application of high technology is revolutionizing product design and development, quality assurance, process control, parts assembly, and cost reduction. This revolution promises to revitalize productivity in our industrial sector, where concern has grown rapidly in the past year over our aging industrial equipment and facilities, the inefficiency of our manufacturing processes, and the high cost of needed research and development.

These developments entail complex social, political, and economic changes. The United States is struggling to deal with the impact of high technology upon its institutions and economy. The scope of education in America, for example, is defined in the context of advanced technological competition. The quality of precollege education in science and math and the number of graduating engineers and scientists are being reexamined for their relevance to new job needs and to industrial competitiveness.

In the workplace, the reliance on advanced technology raises other concerns. The rapidity of technological changes may not permit a natural and relatively painless adjustment of the work force. The balance between jobs lost and jobs created or saved is an issue still to be resolved.

Nontechnological factors also influence our nation's industrial competitiveness. First, universities and industrial firms are forming alliances for research (an approach unique to this country), which will allow the more rapid introduction of new ideas into industry. Second, policymakers are examining the impact of government policies— e.g., antitrust laws, tax incentives, and the allocation of federal research and development funds—upon innovation and competition. Third, industrial leaders are defining the respective roles of government and industry in assuring long-term competitive success.

In addition, the President and Congress are taking significant steps to address the issues that surround U.S. participation in international competition in advanced technologies. President Reagan has appointed a National Commission on Industrial Competitiveness to review and report on the long-term competitiveness of U.S. high-technology industries. He has also introduced legislation to create the Department of International Trade and Industry to help center more attention on international competition and our ability to compete in that environment. Moreover, the Senate Subcommittee on Science, Technology, and Space held hearings in 1983 on the role of technology in promoting industrial competition. During those hearings, a number of major bills (still pending) on this subject were considered.

In addition, the Senate Finance Committee, chaired by Senator Robert Dole, held hearings in April 1983 on a report entitled *International Competition in Advanced Technology: Decisions for America.* That report, included in this book, presents the results of a fourteen-month study by the National Research Council's Panel on Advanced Technology Competition and the Industrialized Allies on the nature of U.S. technology development in the context of international competition. As requested by the National Research Council, the panel focused on an array of issues regarding technology trade and competition between the United States and other major industrialized nations. (Relations with developing countries and the Soviet bloc countries were not considered.) The panel was also asked to recommend fundamental guidelines for national actions that would aid policymakers today and in years to come.

To their deliberations the twenty-two-member panel brought an indispensable diversity of experience and a wealth of expertise in technology, industry, labor, education, economics, and foreign affairs. Meeting monthly, panel members heard expert witnesses from public and private sectors alike and reviewed policy papers and analyses developed in the United States and abroad. In addition, the panel commissioned special studies by experts in relevant fields and discussed the findings and conclusions with their authors.

The panel's report is contained (with minor revisions) in Part One of this book. In it, the panel discusses (1) the nature of advanced technology and its extensive contributions to U.S. economic welfare and military security; (2) the importance of maintaining a strong national capacity for technological innovation, including a vigorous international trade position; and (3) the domestic and international measures required to sustain this effort.

Part Two of this book presents the special studies commissioned by the panel. It includes commentaries prepared by leading economists, specialists in international trade policy, industry executives, and investment finance experts, which focus attention on critical aspects of the overall issue of advanced technology and international trade. In addition, a previously published article by Ralph Gomory, a panel member, is included because the ideas he expressed therein and during panel meetings contributed significantly to the panel's deliberations. These papers do not necessarily represent the final views expressed in the report; they do, however, provide a detailed perspective on many aspects of the topic.

In its report the panel recommends a two-part strategy for fostering greater innovation and competitiveness in advanced technology: to maintain the nation's capacity for technological innovation and to foster an open, healthy international trading system. The concerns and recommendations expressed in the report and the accompanying papers reflect the urgent need seen by the panel members and the other contributors for a greater understanding of issues affecting our industrial competitiveness in high technology and for farsighted and cohesive policy actions to support our competition in international markets.

We wish to express our gratitude to each of the distinguished panel members and to each of the authors who prepared the special studies for the panel's inquiry. We wish to express special thanks to Nancy Gardner, Staff Associate, and Norman Metzger, of the NRC Office of

Government and Public Affairs, for their excellent support. We would also like to thank Paul R. Krugman and Victor K. McElheny of the Massachusetts Institute of Technology for help during the panel's deliberations.

Frank Press
President
National Academy of Sciences
Chairman
National Research Council

Howard W. Johnson
Chairman
Panel on Advanced Technology
   Competition and the
   Industrialized Allies

Anne G. Keatley
Project Director

P A R T   O N E

INTERNATIONAL
COMPETITION IN
ADVANCED TECHNOLOGY

A Consensus Statement Prepared by the
Panel on Advanced Technology Competition
and the Industrialized Allies

Office of International Affairs

National Research Council

Panel on Advanced Technology Competition and the Industrialized Allies

HOWARD W. JOHNSON, Chairman of the Corporation, Massachusetts Institute of Technology, *Chairman*

HARVEY BROOKS, Benjamin Pierce Professor of Technology and Public Policy, Harvard University

ROBERT A. CHARPIE, President, Cabot Corporation

RICHARD N. COOPER, Maurits C. Boas Professor of International Economics, Harvard University

ROBERT A. FULLER, Corporate Vice President, Johnson & Johnson

RALPH E. GOMORY, Vice President and Director of Research, IBM Corporation

NORMAN HACKERMAN, President, Rice University

N. BRUCE HANNAY, Vice President, Research, Bell Laboratories (retired)

THEODORE M. HESBURGH, President, University of Notre Dame

WILLIAM R. HEWLETT, Chairman of the Executive Committee, Hewlett-Packard Company

WILLIAM N. HUBBARD, JR., President, The Upjohn Company

SHIRLEY M. HUFSTEDLER, Partner, Hufstedler Miller Carlson & Beardsley

ROBERT S. INGERSOLL, Former U.S. Ambassador to Japan

CARL KAYSEN, David W. Skinner Professor of Political Economy and Director, Program in Science, Technology & Society, Massachusetts Institute of Technology

ALLEN E. PUCKETT, Chairman and Chief Executive Officer, Hughes Aircraft Company

DAVID V. RAGONE, President, Case Western Reserve University

JOHN S. REED, Vice Chairman, Citibank

WALTER A. ROSENBLITH, Institute Professor, Massachusetts Institute of Technology

ROBERT M. SOLOW, Institute Professor, Department of Economics, Massachusetts Institute of Technology

JOHN E. STEINER, Vice President, Corporate Product Development, The Boeing Company

WILLIAM J. WEISZ, Vice Chairman of the Board, Motorola, Inc.

LEONARD WOODCOCK, Former U.S. Ambassador to China

ANNE G. KEATLEY, Project Director, National Research Council

3

Executive Summary

THE health of U.S. advanced technology industries and their international competitive vigor are central issues in current economic and trade policy debates. The United States, like its major industrialized allies, views the ability to generate and use advanced technologies as essential, both to national economic well-being and to military strength. Many governments—most notably Japan and France—have designed comprehensive national policies to help promote successful technology and trade development in major sectors—telecommunications, biotechnology, computers, microelectronics, and aerospace, for example. The United States has no such defined industrial policy.

U.S. policymakers today must respond not only to a growing anxiety that U.S. leadership in advanced technology and trade is in jeopardy, but also to fears of mounting protectionism. Spurred by global economic ills, domestic unemployment, and loss of traditional markets to newly industrialized countries, governments are attracted to economic nationalism and protectionism—policies that can seriously endanger the international trading system, political alliances, and global technological progress. It is these concerns and the issues surrounding them that are addressed in this consensus statement by the Panel on Advanced Technology Competition and the Industrialized Allies.

The panel discusses the nature of advanced technology and its extensive contributions to U.S. economic welfare and military security; the importance of maintaining a strong national capacity for technological innovation, including a vigorous international trade position; and the domestic and international measures required to sustain this effort.

The panel describes U.S. government and private sector advanced technology policies and practices, as well as those of its major trading partners. Finally, the panel discusses how various national practices may be evaluated and negotiated among nations in support of a

5

healthy mutual international trading system—and what steps the United States must take to protect its interests should international negotiations fail.

While the panel recognizes that contending policy objectives may at times take precedence over the requirements for national strength in technological innovation and trade competitiveness, it concludes that the U.S. advanced technology enterprise has been undervalued in the past in the national scheme of priorities and must be held as one of the country's most valued objectives.

Historical Evolution

The United States' economic and social well-being over the last hundred years has derived substantially from the processes of discovery, invention, and entrepreneurship which Americans have come to value so highly. The nation's capacity for technological innovation became especially apparent in the twenty years following the Second World War, when the United States was acknowledged worldwide as possessing across-the-board technological superiority. Throughout the postwar decades, however, the major industrialized allies combined their recovery from wartime destruction with a rapid rate of technological progress. The result was a progressive narrowing of American technological leadership. While the United States continued to maintain a higher overall productivity level, Europe and Japan enjoyed far higher rates of productivity growth. Today, the allies vie for positions at economic and technological frontiers that at one time seemed reserved for the United States. In many sectors, other industrialized nations are now the first to expand these frontiers.

The United States could not have expected to preserve its vast technological leadership. What it must preserve, however, is a strong capacity for technological innovation that is vital to the future growth of the entire American economy. Domestic weaknesses and damaging practices of other nations can endanger this innovative capacity, the basis for advanced technology development and international trade competitiveness. The United States must now adopt measures designed to preserve this vital capacity.

Technology and the Nation's Economic Well-Being and Military Security

The national capacity to generate and use advanced technology is fundamental to the economic well-being and military security of the United States. Advanced technologies serve to increase productivity in services, manufacturing, and agriculture. The United States has the potential for a new economic surge fueled by advanced technology—a dramatic increase in the productivity of workers utilizing new information-processing technologies, new materials, and new manufacturing technologies. In addition, the U.S. positive trade balance in technology-intensive products and services contributes to domestic employment and economic health.

The nation's innovative capacity is vital to military as well as economic security. A major fraction of defense hardware is procured from technology-intensive companies. Advanced weapons employ frontier electronics systems, and verification methods fundamental to arms control agreements rely on advanced technologies. The interrelationships between the U.S. commercial and military advanced technology systems are complex, but it is clear that military systems rely on a strong civilian industrial base and that many commercial efforts benefit from defense and space research and development expenditures and procurement.

National Capacity for Innovation

Our capacity for technological innovation is commonly perceived in terms of industrial sectors—microelectronics, computers, new materials, robots, telecommunications, aerospace, and, most recently, biotechnology. This list is, in fact, a transitory one—changing over time. A new list may supersede this one in a decade or two. The nation's innovative capacity should not be thought of only in terms of specific products; it should be understood as the continuous capability, widely diffused throughout the economy, to produce and put to use pioneering technological resources.

This national innovative capacity is manifested primarily in a system of interrelated activities leading to commercial sales of products, most frequently referred to as the innovation process. This dynamic system not only involves basic research and product development, but also encompasses manufacture, marketing, and distribution. Each part of the process must function effectively to ensure success.

Maintaining Technological Strength

The United States' capacity for technological innovation and competitiveness in world markets is an essential national resource, requiring a sophisticated and thorough understanding of the innovation process—what it is, how it works, what influences it, and what is necessary for its strength. Maintaining a world-class research structure is essential in the effort to expand technological frontiers. Research is a vital first requisite, but it is only one part of a complex, interwoven process. Product planning requires knowledge of new technologies in the research phases; development of commercially successful products requires links with marketing assessments; and successful commercialization pays for the next round of technological advance.

The innovation process, then, is an interlocking system that must be strong throughout. Its requirements include technologically sophisticated managers, quality research personnel, and a technically competent labor force. The process of innovation also requires a healthy supply of capital—both venture capital for starting up new enterprises and growth capital for established firms. Large-scale economies utilizing world markets are necessary to support succeeding rounds of technological advance.

A more elusive but major influence on the innovation process may be the government's role in establishing a climate that fosters entrepreneurial risk-taking. Stable, informed government policies can lessen uncertainty for innovative entrepreneurs.

Government's Role

In the U.S. economy, institutional arrangements to foster advanced technology operate primarily in the private sector—in small innovative firms, national and multinational companies, banking and financial communities, and the research universities. The United

States has had no national plan nor even a loose coordinating mechanism linking the efforts of these private actors to federal government actions.

The government's primary role in fostering the nation's innovative capacity has been in education and support of basic research. There is, however, a range of government instruments to address broad national objectives that affect various stages of the innovation process, including market development. These instruments—which are compatible with our culture and style (as total government-industry coordination in the manner often attributed to Japan is not)—include tax policies fostering research, development and investment in production facilities, patent laws, regulation and deregulation, antitrust measures, export/import bank loans, and government procurement, among others. Beyond these measures, uncoordinated actions taken by various governmental agencies, designed to serve other purposes, affect the innovation process—unintentionally helping it in some instances, but hindering it in others. The nation's capacity to perform well in advanced technology and trade is, in fact, affected by decisions that are made independently, inter alia, by the Food and Drug Administration, the Environmental Protection Agency, the antitrust division of the Department of Justice, the departments of Commerce, State, Agriculture, and Defense, the National Security Assistant, the Special Trade Representative, the President's Science Advisor, the National Aeronautics and Space Administration, the National Science Foundation, and the National Institutes of Health. Yet the heads of these executive branch entities rarely if ever have joined together to consider the totality of their separate actions on the nation's advanced technology capabilities and international competitiveness—either what it is or what it should be.

If the United States is to maintain its innovative vitality over time, it is essential that executive and congressional policymakers periodically evaluate both the U.S. comparative international trade position and the health of the nation's innovative capacity. They should do so by means of a broad analysis, conducted at cabinet level, of all the variables impinging on our capacity to innovate—both domestic and foreign. These periodic assessments would require support by a continuing source of expertise drawn both from within the government and from outside.

Reviews should be comprehensive. They should assess:

- the impact of U.S. government policies on the nation's innovative capacity and international trade competitiveness;
- the nation's standing with regard to research and development, manufacturing, and marketing;
- the effectiveness (in comparison with other countries) of U.S. elementary and secondary educational systems, postsecondary institutions, and continuing education programs, especially in maintaining and renewing our technological and scientific manpower and knowledge;
- the trends in our comparative international trade standing; and
- the policies of major trading partners and their effects on the United States and the international trading system.

The process of periodic evaluation could result in recommendations, at the national level, to coordinate actions across agencies, to rationalize government policies, or to ensure consistency over time in government practices, as well as recommendations at the transnational level to initiate coordinated negotiations or actions with industrialized trading partners and allies. In addition, the assessment process should stimulate Congressional hearings to seek the views of leaders from industry, labor, and other sectors. An opportunity for comprehensive and coherent review of U.S. innovative capacity and international trade competitiveness by representatives of all sectors contributing to it should help to elevate technological innovation goals in the scheme of national priorities.

Management's Responsibilities

A coordinated decision-making process is essential, but the nation's performance in advanced technology development and trade will be determined in large part by the efforts of individual firms. Successful firms are those whose managers have long-range vision of how technology affects the growth of their business. They understand the state of technology in their industry worldwide; they respond to the international climate when planning for research, development, manufacturing, and marketing; and they are open to developing new institutional arrangements to foster technological growth—such as industry-university research relationships, cooperative research ventures among groups of firms, or consortia to seek information and ideas systematically from abroad.

Advanced Technology Trade Practices

U.S. firms face a mixed international trading system in which they are operating independently as private entities, yet are frequently competing with foreign firms, singly or in consortia, that either are government entities or have strong government backing. This mixed international trading environment often effectively places an American company in competition against a country. By "targeting" certain advanced technology sectors, a country may provide its firms with a range of support—from direct and indirect subsidies for research and manufacturing through help in penetrating foreign markets. Such practices are not within the U.S. arsenal of policies. Traditionally, U.S. philosophy has stressed private sector initiatives within a competitive framework.

U.S. firms are understandably concerned about the tactics other countries use to develop markets—both at home and abroad. American firms have difficulty penetrating European and Japanese markets when they are faced with intentional collective actions excluding them. At the same time, too, U.S. businesses must compete with European and Japanese firms for new and potentially lucrative emerging-nation markets. Often foreign firms have strong support from their home governments, an advantage U.S. firms do not enjoy to a comparable extent. To lose out in this competition could be extremely damaging, not only for American advanced technology industries, but eventually, because of intersectoral linkages, for other areas of the economy as well.

There is considerable dispute among the industrialized allies regarding which trade practices are acceptable and which are not. Actions that are consistent with one nation's traditions and attitudes may be inimical to another. Friction is exacerbated worldwide by current conditions of slow growth, excess capacity, obsolete plants, and lingering inflation. These conditions make politically more difficult and financially more costly structural adjustments that would shift financial, manpower, and other resources from less to more com-

11

petitive industries. Many nations are suffering from record unemployment levels that cause significant domestic political problems.

U.S. Objectives

U.S. objectives in advanced technology trade must take into account both the needs of our own industries and those of our principal allies. Innovation proceeds most rapidly and efficiently when new products have access to the widest possible markets, thus spreading the costs and risks of innovation over more units and generating the cash flow for follow-on improvements and fresh innovation.

The United States should negotiate in international forums to secure the openness of world markets to innovative entrepreneurs wherever they may be based and to discourage large-scale distortions of free markets. Such a policy is required both to preserve the U.S. position as a major source of innovation and to ease growing tensions among the industrialized allies, tensions that threaten not only international economic and political management, but also mutually beneficial cooperation in science and technology.

Nowhere is our national welfare more interwoven with that of our allies than in the fields of science cooperation and high-technology trade. The costs and risks of protectionist policies and market fragmentation are probably greater than in almost any other economic field except energy. Paradoxically, the international coordination of trade practices is more backward in advanced technology than in many other fields at a time when both nations and regions within nations are looking more and more to advanced technology as a primary source of economic salvation.

Negotiations Required

Protectionist pressures are strong in today's very difficult economic times. Furthermore, international negotiations on trading practices are complicated by differing viewpoints among allies on what national practices are acceptable. Attempts to sort practices into acceptable and unacceptable categories have been only moderately successful, but such attempts should continue. Progress may be slow and agreements difficult, but the health of the international trading system is at stake. Negotiations should consider the consequences of actions and place value on maintaining open markets, for they reward innovators by offering innovative products globally.

To foster healthy, mutual competition in advanced technology is a primary objective. Negotiations, though protracted, will serve the interests of the United States and her allies better than precipitous actions. Proposals for legislative action to protect advanced technology industries, currently before the Congress, require careful analysis and consideration in light of the findings of this report.

Cooperation among industry, government, labor, university, finance, and other sectors is essential in dealing with these exceedingly complex problems in technology and trade. Most difficult will be those circumstances in which U.S. capacities are well nurtured and strong, yet key industries essential to the national welfare are nonetheless endangered. Vulnerability could develop because of successful aggressive policies of our allies, which individually may or may not be considered as unfair, but which together endanger U.S. major technology industries and fundamental advanced technology capacity deemed essential to economic well-being and military security. Where such broad national resources are in jeopardy, the United States must take action.

A first step is to seek to renegotiate multilaterally agreed rules in forums such as the GATT in order to establish clearer guidelines for government actions in high-technology sectors. A basic requirement of such negotiations would be that countries, including the United States, be prepared to consider altering traditional practices.

When there is a specific threat to U.S. interests from a particular country's government policies, the U.S. government should initiate bilateral consultations within the framework of GATT and other appropriate multilateral institutions. The goal of such negotiations would be to reach agreements on a time scale that would prevent or reverse damage to U.S. capacity for technological innovation. If these bilateral consultations are unsuccessful in resolving issues, the U.S. government should utilize formal multilateral dispute settlement procedures to seek a resolution. If those procedures in turn fail or if the threat of damage is imminent, the United States would be required to take unilateral action to protect the national interest as a step of last resort.

Conclusions

- The United States must act now to preserve its basic capacity to develop and use economically advanced technology. This innovative capacity is essential for the self-renewal and well-being of the economy and the nation's military security. Trade in advanced technology products and services will contribute enormously to our economic health. Advanced technology products and processes not only permeate the economy, increasing productivity, but also form the basis of modern defense hardware.

- The nation's capacity for technological innovation is vulnerable both from domestic weaknesses and from damaging practices of other nations. Measures designed to maintain this vital aspect of the American economy within a healthy international trading system will include both domestic actions and international negotiations.

- Effective actions require a sound understanding of the nature of innovative capacity and of the innovation process through which it is primarily manifest. Innovative capacity is the capability, widely diffused throughout the economy, to produce continuously forefront technological resources, and to use those resources for the national benefit. The innovation process includes not only basic research and development but also production, marketing, and distribution in domestic and foreign markets. Each part of the process must be sound for success.

- Some of the elements that support our nation's innovative capabilities include a strong national research base, technically educated manpower and a technically literate population, capable and farsighted industrial managers, a financial base that provides capital to both new and established firms, and sizable markets. Essential, too, are a national understanding of and attention to advanced technology as a vital contributor to the national welfare.

- The U.S. government has in effect a range of policies and practices including tax policies, patent laws, regulation and deregulation, antitrust measures, export/import bank loans, government procurement, and others that, although designed to serve other national objectives, also affect the U.S. technological enterprise and international trade position. These policies and practices and the other domestic and international elements affecting U.S. technology and trade must be well understood by senior policymakers. If viewed in ensemble, existing government instruments may become powerful means to support U.S. technology and trade interests.

· Responsibility for improving U.S. performance in advanced technology and trade rests to a large degree with the individual firm and its management. Successful managers increasingly will have to be cognizant of frontier technologies as they build businesses and compete in an international world.

· Our major industrialized allies—most notably Japan and France—have designed comprehensive national policies to help ensure successful technology and trade development in major sectors. Thus, individual U.S. firms often find themselves competing internationally, not with firms acting alone, but with countries or with consortia of firms with country backing.

· There is considerable dispute among industrialized allies regarding which practices are acceptable and which are not. Efforts to evaluate practices are protracted and difficult, but essential.

Recommendations

Accordingly, the panel recommends the following:

· Advanced technology development and trade must be considered as among the highest priorities of the nation. These vital interests must be well understood domestically and conveyed to our trading partners. The United States must initiate a two-part strategy: to maintain the nation's capacity for technological innovation and to foster an open healthy international trading system.

· The federal government should initiate a biennial, cabinet-level review that comprehensively assesses U.S. trade competitiveness and the health of the nation's innovative capacity in both relative and absolute terms. This review should consider the nation's overall performance: the private sector activities and the totality of government actions on technology and trade, as well as the effects of other governments' practices. These assessments would consider the strength of key technological sectors across all stages of the innovation process—research, development, manufacture, and distribution. In addition, assessments would evaluate broad elements as they affect innovation, such as the macroeconomic environment, regulatory policy, patent policy, and antitrust policy. Careful attention would be given to maintaining the health and effectiveness of both university- and industry-based research, education, and training. The cabinet-level review should be supported by a continuing mechanism that would draw on expertise both from within the government and from outside.

- Managers of private firms must be cognizant of technological trends as they make renewed efforts to build businesses and compete in an international context. Managers should consider new institutional arrangements—the growing, mutually supportive, industry-university research relationships, cooperative research ventures among groups of firms, or consortia to seek information and ideas systematically from abroad.

- Internationally, the United States should negotiate in existing forums to encourage a healthy mutual trading system. This should include continued efforts to evaluate national trade practices and to agree on criteria for acceptability. An objective must be to encourage open markets and healthy competition.

- Countries, including the United States, throughout negotiations should be prepared to alter fundamental policies so that each country may maintain advanced technology capacities fundamental to its individual welfare.

- The United States should review the content and application of its trade laws to ensure that U.S. industries can obtain timely and meaningful trade and/or other relief in the U.S. market when imports from particular countries, based on unreasonable or excessive foreign industrial policies, threaten them.

- If key technology industries essential to national economic welfare and military security are considered endangered by the actions of another country, even with all necessary domestic efforts to strengthen these sectors, then the United States should negotiate with the other country requesting immediate relief. Negotiations should take place first in existing forums, explaining our country's vital interest in preserving advanced technology capacity. If such mechanisms prove ineffective or too slow to prevent damage to essential U.S. capabilities, then the United States should negotiate directly with the country in question. If those bilateral negotiations fail or if the threat of damage is imminent, the United States should take immediate unilateral actions as a step of last resort.

Introduction

T HIS consensus statement has two themes:

- The requirement that the United States maintain strong domestic capacity for technological innovation—to benefit its domestic economy, its national security, and its competition for global markets in technological products and services.
- The need to reduce trade frictions that trouble economic and political relations among the major industrialized allies—principally, Canada, the Federal Republic of Germany, France, Japan, the United Kingdom, and the United States.

The leading industrial nations believe that their future economic growth depends on their abilities to create advanced technologies and to sell the resultant products and processes in a global market. Consequently, international trade in advanced technology is a high priority.

International competition has led to concern within the United States about our capacity to create advanced technologies and to develop them into commercially successful products in international and U.S. markets. Competition also has led to frictions among countries because of their differing national practices in supporting development and international trade.

Frictions among the industrialized allies may be inevitable now that many nations can adopt or innovate frontier technologies and can manufacture and market advanced technology products. Realistically, the United States cannot expect to maintain the overwhelming market share in advanced technologies that it had during much of the postwar period. The United States, however, must preserve a strong capacity for technological innovation that is vital to the entire American economy and to its growth. The United States must adopt measures designed to preserve this vital aspect of the American economy within a healthy international trading system.

Trade frictions among the allies have developed in part because

18

of the measures that different countries use to promote their advanced technologies. There are charges that some countries use "nontariff" barriers and other market-distorting practices to exclude the products of other countries from their home markets, charges of "dumping" (selling below cost) advanced technology products in order to gain rapidly a substantial share of a foreign market, charges that foreign companies are capable of underbidding American manufacturers through major subsidization by their governments, and charges that governments use so-called side inducements to capture sales in third-country markets. These perceptions, whatever their validity, weaken the bonds among the industrialized allies and may threaten the economic and military strength of all countries of the alliance.

Government and industry are partners in many countries, each with a role in developing globally competitive advanced technologies. In the United States, the private sector traditionally has carried the responsibility for trade development. One result is that many American companies perceive an international system in which they are competing not against individual foreign companies acting alone, but rather against foreign companies and company groups operating in concert with their governments.

While differences in governmental and industrial relations among various countries are to be expected, there is a marked difference between the American style and that of other countries. That difference leads to the prevalent American perception that the forms of guidance and direct support that other governments offer specific industries is "unfair," in the sense of distorting the free market and making it difficult for American companies to compete on equal terms. Ill feelings are exacerbated by the depressed economic environment. The U.S. economic picture currently includes unemployment that exceeds 10 percent, a recorded rate of utilization of our industrial capacity of only 70 percent, depressed corporate profits, and widespread business bankruptcies. Comparable conditions prevail in other industrialized countries. Industrial production in France, Germany, and the United Kingdom declined in 1982. The unemployment rates in Canada and the United Kingdom are over 12 percent and are projected to exceed 13 percent in 1983. In Japan, export market demand declined substantially in 1982, and only a modest growth in export volumes is predicted for 1983.[1] As a result

19

of these unfavorable economic conditions, orders for new production are depressed, and competition—including competition from imports—is exceptionally stiff. The U.S. trade position has been made more vulnerable by the very strong dollar relative to other currencies, as well as by the 1982 high U.S. interest rates.

In our approach to advanced technology competition in international trade, we have tried to see beyond this current economic trauma. Certainly much of the distress that American firms now feel arises from these general economic conditions. But we believe that some of the problems the country faces in advanced technology go deeper than these adverse economic conditions and need to be addressed directly.

As stated above, each country creates different policies and stratagems to enhance the global competitiveness of its advanced technology industries. Advanced technology sectors are important to the United States and other industrialized countries because their future economic growth depends in large part on the dissemination of advanced technology throughout their economies. In addition, advanced technology industries contribute significantly to productivity growth and product innovation. In the United States, ten industries[2] that in 1980 accounted for only 5 percent of U.S. employment and 13 percent of the value of manufacturing product shipments were responsible for more than 60 percent of total private industrial R&D spending. These industries employed more than 25 percent of the nation's scientists and engineers. In addition, these ten industries had a $31 billion favorable balance of trade. During the 1970s, labor productivity in these industries grew more than six times as fast as in the business sector as a whole. Growth in advanced technology industries benefits the entire economy because it results in rapid employment growth in other industries.[3]

Measures of shares of world exports for products and services embodying advanced technology indicate a deterioration in the U.S. competitive position. Between 1962 and 1980, the U.S. share of the industrialized countries' exports of advanced technology products declined from 30 to 24 percent. During the same period, Japan tripled its industrial country export market share, while West Germany's and France's shares increased slightly.[4] Underlying these trends in the aggregate are significant changes in individual technologies. In electronics, particularly semiconductors, Japan has made

20

dramatic inroads into the U.S. market;[5] in aircraft, the European consortium Airbus Industrie has captured a substantial share of the commercial jetliner market in which U.S. firms held a 97 percent share in 1976.[6]

These changes stem from many elements that have affected international trade at different periods—for example, the postwar renaissance of European science, technology, and industry; long-term structural changes; and the well-planned effort by the Japanese to raise the technological intensity of their economy. Other factors contributing to a diminishing of U.S. global market shares include the extraordinarily high value of the dollar relative to other countries in 1980 and other years. There is some evidence, for example, that the pattern of trade tensions between Japan and the United States has tracked exchange rate developments.[7] In 1970–71, 1976–77, and again in 1981, a strong dollar against the yen produced large favorable trade surpluses for Japan. In the first two instances, subsequent appreciation of the yen against the dollar reduced the imbalance after a couple of years. In recent months, there has been some strengthening of the yen, but it is too soon to know if it has gone far enough, or how much of the current Japanese surplus will be eliminated, or how any improvement will be distributed across industries.

This setting of intensifying competition, rising frictions among allies, and, for the moment, a bleak economic outlook frames this consensus statement by the Panel on Advanced Technology Competition and the Industrialized Allies.

The panel discusses the extensive contributions of advanced technology to U.S. economic welfare and military security; the importance of maintaining a strong national capacity for technological innovation, including a vigorous international trade position; and the domestic and international measures required for this effort. It describes the many variables affecting the nation's advanced technology enterprise, including U.S. government and private-sector policies and practices, as well as the actions of major trading partners. Finally, the panel discusses how various national practices may be evaluated and negotiated among nations in support of a healthy mutual international trading system and what steps the United States must take to protect its interests should international negotiations fail.

The panel recognizes that the United States has many domestic and foreign policy objectives in addition to the requirements for national strength in technological innovation and trade competitiveness and that these, at times, may take precedence with regard to allocation of resources and policymaking. It concludes, however, that the U.S. advanced technology enterprise has been undervalued in the past in the national scheme of priorities and must be held as one of the country's most valued objectives.

NOTES

[1] Organisation for Economic Co-operation and Development, *OECD Economic Outlook*, No. 32 (Paris: OECD, 1982), pp. 12, 15, 35.

[2] Electrical equipment and components; aircraft and parts; computers and office equipment; optical and medical instruments; drugs and medicines; industrial chemicals; agricultural chemicals; professional and scientific instruments; engines and turbines; and plastic and synthetic materials. "An Assessment of U.S. Competitiveness in High-Technology Industries," a study prepared for the Cabinet Council on Commerce and Trade, revised draft, October 1982, p. 4. Statistical evidence on U.S. competitiveness in advanced technology relies on the isolation of *technology-intensive* industries, defined as industries that have either high R&D-to-sales ratios or industries with a high proportion of scientists and engineers in their work force. Such evidence is useful, but it must be used with caution for several reasons:

- The match between *technologies* and *industries* is not perfect. Large parts of an apparently advanced technology industry may involve routine production of traditional products; on the other hand, seemingly "low-technology" industries have components that are at the forefront of technical advance.

- The classification of technologies as advanced ought to be, in principle, a dynamic one, since it largely depends on how new the technology is. Today's advanced technology becomes tomorrow's traditional method; on the other hand, an industry that is low-tech now may become a technological leader in the future. Statistical comparison based on a fixed list of technology-intensive industries are, therefore, potentially misleading.

- All available statistical evidence focuses exclusively on manufacturing. Yet, service exports should in many cases be regarded as technology-intensive. This applies both to financial services and to the overseas earnings of multinational firms, much of which can be viewed as a return to technology.

[3] Ibid., pp. 4–5, 29.

[4] Ibid., p. 10.

[5] For a discussion of the nature of Japan's competitive challenge in semiconductors, see Semiconductor Industry Association, *The International Microelectronics Challenge: The American Response by the Industry, the Universities, and the Government* (Cupertino, Calif.: SIA, 1981), pp. 33–35.

[6] Airbus Industrie orders represented 3 percent of the total market for commercial aircraft in 1976 and 32 percent in 1980. Aerospace Industries Association of America, Inc., *The Challenge of Foreign Competition to the U.S. Jet Transport Manufacturing Industry*, an ad hoc study project of the Civil Aviation Advisory Group, Aerospace Technical Council (Washington, D.C.: Aerospace Research Center, 1982), p. 41.

[7] C. Fred Bergsten, "What to do About the U.S.-Japan Economic Conflict?" *Foreign Affairs*, Summer 1982, pp. 1065–1067.

O N E

Advanced Technology: Its Nature and
Its Importance to the United States

THE nation's capacity for technological innovation is an essential national resource that permeates and strengthens the entire economy. Advanced technology products and processes are central to a range of domestic economic activities and serve to increase productivity. In addition, advanced technology is vital to the military security of the United States and, thus, to the defense of the Western Alliance.

What Is Advanced Technology?

Examples of advanced technology industries are extensive, yet changing. They include microelectronics, computers, new materials, robotics, telecommunications, aerospace, and biotechnology. The list of technologies deemed "advanced" changes over time. A new list may supersede this one in a decade or two.

Integrated circuit chips perhaps best illustrate advanced technology's broad impact. Their role is to process data and signals—and hence information, a capacity that is critical not only to all scientific and technological fields, but increasingly to all economic sectors. Microelectronics has become a primary component of technological advance.

It is misleading, however, to describe advanced technology through its products—the computer or the laser. The essential national resource is the capacity for technological innovation—the ability to continuously discover, refine, and produce frontier technologies and to use those technologies throughout the industrial, agricultural, and military enterprises.

The Innovation Process

The capacity for technological innovation is manifested in the innovation process, an integrated complex system. Competition in advanced technology is not simply a matter of generating the best ideas. New ideas are only one essential part—among several crucial components—of what is necessary for a nation to be technologically competitive. The innovation process includes not only research and development, but also manufacture, marketing, and distribution. It may be described roughly in four parts:

Research—whether in a university setting, in research institutes, in government laboratories, or in industry—generates new scientific knowledge and new ideas for application. One innovation leads to another by suggesting new directions for further technological investment. In industry, company interests usually dictate research; in universities and research institutes, individual scientists choose whatever scientific leads they deem both important and capable of attracting financial support.

Development translates a new discovery or idea into a usable product aimed at a defined market demand. It encompasses the steps between research and completion of the design of a product. It includes a *validation* phase, where elements emerge from a research environment to one having risk low enough to permit their use in a product, and an *application* phase which integrates such elements into a product design suitable for production. The former frequently proceeds before the application product is known, and certainly long before it is defined. The latter phase, application, occurs after the product is known. It can include prototype or pilot scale tests on either product or process. Development responds both to research results and to feedback from the marketplace.

Manufacturing or production takes the product or process from a single prototype to quantity production that promises the consumer reliable quality and controlled cost. The line between development and manufacturing is expressed in the comment that it's always possible to make *one* of anything; regular production demands reliability, competitive costs, serviceability, often retooling of the manufacturing plants, setting and enforcing criteria for suppliers, and more.

Distribution entails marketing, delivery, customer training, and support services. It addresses the requirements of the consumer in using the product.

The innovation process is a dynamic and intricately interrelated system: there are interactions and feedbacks among the four stages. Early efforts in development, for example, may reveal gaps in basic knowledge that require the launching of a new research effort, or user experience with a new product may call for redesign at the development level to better adapt the product to consumer needs. Thus successful innovation is characterized by constant rethinking, adaptation, and organizational learning; only rarely is there an orderly, logical process that can be completely foreseen in advance. Indeed, the difference between success and failure often depends precisely on sufficient flexibility and "fast footwork" in changing course to respond to new information.

Why Is Advanced Technology Important to the United States?

Advanced technology has been called the "fuel" of the economy. New technologies—such as microelectronics, computer-aided design, computer-aided manufacturing, robotics, and advanced computer capabilities—spark a surge of economic growth by increasing worker productivity. Military security relies on pioneering technologies for defense systems and for verification of limitations on weapons systems specified in arms control agreements. Advanced technology is perceived as a strong part of our national self-image: the United States is thought to excel through "Yankee ingenuity."

Advanced Technology and National Security

National defense relies on advanced technology products for sophisticated military hardware. Technologies used in defense systems can often be exploited for commercial purposes. Very-high-speed integrated circuits, digital telecommunications, and new high-performance materials all were developed for defense or space purposes yet now have commercial spin-offs.

New processing and fabrication methods may also apply to both military and civilian efforts. A goal of the manufacturing technology program of the Air Force was to demonstrate that computers can reduce cost in all phases of manufacturing aircraft and thereby enhance manufacturing flexibility. The driving force behind this program was the high cost of relatively small production runs typical of military aircraft, but civilian aircraft manufacture benefited as well.[1] The Defense Department's Very-High-Speed Integrated Circuit program (VHSIC),[2] designed to produce electronic devices that are faster and more reliable than circuits now in use, is being developed for the military but is expected to have important commercial uses.[3]

Military sources of R&D support, however, do carry some disadvantages for the commercial sector. Classifications, export controls, and rigid criteria for research, as well as the drawing away by the military of scientific and engineering personnel, sometimes inhibit, rather than promote, commercial developments.

Advantages flow from commercial research to the military as well. The military's ability to obtain the technology and hardware it requires often stems from the development and production strength that contractor companies have derived from competition in civilian markets. Healthy competition among companies selling semiconductors, lasers, commercial aircraft, computers, and other advanced technology products to a mass market, for example, sped the development of useful military applications of these products. The greater the civilian sales, the lower the per-unit R&D cost for both civilian and military requirements.

The nation must retain both excellence and self-sufficiency in military technology. To that end, a strong domestic technological enterprise is essential.

Advanced Technology and Trade

A U.S. positive trade balance in technology-intensive products and services contributes not only to employment, but also to the general health of the nation's economy. In 1980, advanced technology prod-

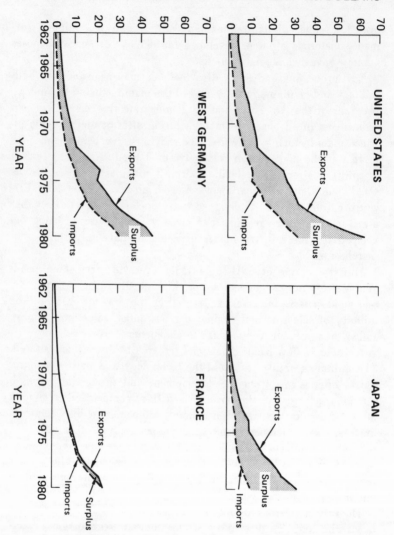

FIGURE 1   Relative changes in the balance of trade in high-technology products: United States, Japan, West Germany, and France, 1962 to 1980. *SOURCE: U.S. Department of Commerce, International Trade Administration, from U.N. Series D Trade Data, as reported in "An Assessment of U.S. Competitiveness in High-Technology Industries," a study prepared for the Working Group on High-Technology Industries of the Cabinet Council on Commerce and Trade, final draft, May 19, 1982.*

28

ucts showed a positive trade balance of $31 billion, compared to a deficit of more than $50 billion for all other manufactured goods.[4]

The U.S. currently holds the highest market share of the industrialized countries' exports of high-technology products. That share declined, however, from 30 percent in 1962 to 22 percent in 1978 and has increased only marginally since.[5] Figure 1 shows that in absolute terms, the U.S. trade balance in high-technology products increased over eightfold from 1962 to 1980. The statistic is less heartening when compared to the trade balances of Japan and West Germany during the same period. Their positive balances increased more than two-hundredfold and ninefold, respectively, starting from a much lower 1962 base.

Advanced Technologies—Core Technologies in the Economy

The benefits of advanced technologies extend beyond the military and trade spheres to virtually all sectors of the American economy, including the service sector, manufacturing, and agriculture. Electronics is one core technology arena in the form of integrated circuitry of increasingly higher density, digital devices for communication, an enlarging array of computers, and increasing sophistication in "user-friendly" software. Another emerging core technology, embraced by the umbrella term "biotechnology," includes not only modern-day fermentation techniques using recombinant DNA methodology, but also new biological techniques for the manufacture of hormones and drugs.

Core technologies have far-reaching influence upon the state of the American economy. The rapidly improving performance and falling costs of these advanced technology products are key to rising productivity. In ten years, productivity in advanced technology industries has risen 5.6 percent, compared to 0.9 percent for business generally—a sixfold difference.[6] In addition, productivity in mature industries may be increased through the application of advanced technology throughout the manufacturing and distribution processes. Also, seemingly low-technology industries such as ceramics or glassware have components that are at the forefront of technical advance.

The diffusion of advanced technologies throughout the economy can be subtle. For example, the service sector in America is growing. Employment in service industries (banking, health care, insurance,

29

transportation, utilities, etc.) between 1940 and 1980 grew from 46 percent of total employment to 68 percent.[7] Pressured by the need to improve productivity and to serve a growing population, service industries draw increasingly on new technologies: electronic tellers, word processors, and small stand-alone computers have become commonplace only a few years after their introduction.

Need for National Attention

The advanced technology enterprise has special characteristics that strengthen its claim to national attention. Even small companies can be technologically innovative and economically viable, but a new innovative product is subject to cumulatively increasing returns to scale over time, that is, with research and production experience there is a reduction in average cost. On the other hand, temporary setbacks, if severe, can cripple future efficiency by starving the scientific and technological roots of the innovation process. It is easier to stay at the frontier than to achieve it.

Were the United States to lose its capacity to innovate core technologies, it might still benefit from foreign innovations, just as other countries have benefited from advanced technologies originating in the United States. It is the innovating country, however, that has the best access to new technologies and, thus, the best opportunities to use them. The rapidity of change in many important technological fields requires knowledge of technological innovation in progress and immediate access to new technologies. Without that knowledge and access, a country's capacity to plan for new products would lag behind those of the innovating country. The effects of such a lag could be felt throughout the U.S. economy, affecting not only advanced technology industries, but also others that require the products of these industries for advancement, including the now widespread service industries.

Advanced Technology and the Nation's Future

The social fabric of a nation is knitted by its citizens' common purposes and widely shared beliefs in the integrity and stature of their country and in the belief in a strong future. Throughout our history, Americans have believed in the capacity of the United States to adapt to new circumstances, to use native skills and resourcefulness—"Yankee ingenuity"—to create practical objects of commercial value. That belief endures as a national assumption that the country will continue to expand technological frontiers and thus ensure the well-being of its people. The capacity of Americans to innovate and to adapt to change is thus important to sustain, as much for the national optimism as for the technological benefits that flow from technological prowess.

NOTES

[1] See National Research Council, *Innovation and Transfer of U.S. Air Force Manufacturing Technology: Three Case Studies* (Washington, D.C.: National Academy Press, 1981), pp. 6–18.

[2] For descriptions of the scope and goals of the VHSIC program, see Jim Martin, "Very-High-Speed Integrated Circuits—Into the Second Generation, Part I: The Birth of a Program," *Military Electronics/Countermeasures*, December 1981, pp. 52–58, 71–73.

[3] National Research Council, *An Assessment of the Impact of the Department of Defense Very-High-Speed Integrated Circuit Program* (Washington, D.C.: National Academy Press, 1982), p. 13.

[4] "An Assessment of U.S. Competitiveness," p. 44.

[5] Ibid., p. A-38.

[6] Ibid., p. 45.

[7] "Service sector" is defined in the broadest sense to encompass all enterprises not engaged in the production of goods. Unpublished data from the Department of Labor, Bureau of Labor Statistics.

TWO

National Policies Affecting
Advanced Technology Capacity
and Competition

THE innovation process, as we have seen, embraces research, development, manufacturing, marketing, and distribution. A wide variety of government policies affect this process—those explicitly intended to strengthen it, such as federal support of basic research; those framed for a broader impact, such as the nation's fiscal and monetary policies; and those aimed at other objectives that may unintentionally adversely affect the process, such as export controls. In this chapter we consider how national policies affect a nation's advanced technology capacity and international trade position.

Many governments have designed comprehensive policies to ensure successful technology and trade development. Their efforts span the whole of the innovation process. The U.S. system supports basic research applicable to broad national goals but does not systematically support the other parts of the process leading to commercial sales. Responsibility for product development, production, marketing, and distribution are left to the individual firm. This system of free enterprise has worked remarkably well. However, as other governments coordinate—and provide increasing support to—their advanced technology industries, American firms find themselves competing internationally with government-aided firms or groups of firms. U.S. industry feels burdened by an unfair disadvantage.

Basic Research

Governmental support of basic research may serve broad national needs—for national defense, for food production, for medical care, and for energy availability—but current spending on basic research is only tenuously linked to current competition for markets for advanced technologies.

Investment in basic research is a capital investment with a payback period measured in decades rather than years. Because the results of basic research are quickly available globally, governmental support does not spark international conflict. Each country's research benefits others. Indeed, the United States is a major beneficiary not only of its own research but of the research abroad as well.

Strength in a nation's research infrastructure, however, is no guarantee of successful technological competition. A country may lead in basic science, but lag in the process of making innovative ideas commercially profitable. On the other hand, a country may lag in research, but draw on research conducted abroad as a base for creating commercially successful advanced technologies. Japan has followed this strategy with remarkable success. Japanese leaders recognize, however, that an economically and technologically advanced country must develop a strong domestic research base in order to excel at making world-class technological advances.[1] France, too, has chosen to increase support of basic research. The United States has one of the strongest research bases in the world, but this base is not invulnerable. Federal support for basic research rose rapidly in the United States from 1960 to 1968 discounting inflation, but has increased only marginally against inflation since then (Figure 2).

Applied Research and Development

National practices diverge more sharply with regard to support for applied research and development than with regard to basic research. The three most prominent positions favoring some support follow.

First, a traditional U.S. position held by many industrial leaders and recent administrations is skeptical of any government effort to

33

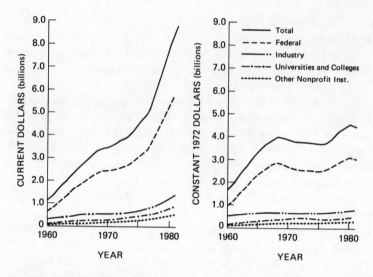

FIGURE 2 Basic research expenditures by source, 1960 to 1981. Estimates are shown for 1979–81. GNP implicit price deflators used to convert current dollars to constant 1972 dollars.

SOURCE: National Science Foundation, Science Indicators 1980.

select particular sectors of industrial R&D for support. It holds rather that decisions on investing in development and the subsequent stages of industrial innovation are best made by private industry. This view, however, does espouse government support through tax credits for industry-determined research.

Another view, occasionally argued in the United States but practiced primarily in other countries, suggests that the diffuse benefits, or "spillovers," of technological development warrant federal targeted support to particular technologies. It is argued that such support leads to commercially successful products—indeed, that favorable technological spillovers are likely even if the targeted products or processes are unsuccessful.

A third position, taken by some foreign governments, is that government support is warranted for those technologies for which there is a national need and in which the private market would tend to underinvest, either because of high risks and costs or because the benefits likely to result from research and development are not easily captured. Certainly, in the United States and elsewhere, defense and those space technologies where the government is the prime customer receive full governmental research and development support.

Production

France and Japan, among others, believe that government support for new technologies should in part assure production of the new industrial products. Proponents of this view stress that experience gained in manufacturing is crucial, that there is no clean break between development and production, and that, in any case, intervention by governments in advanced technology is justified by enhancing employment and making broad contributions to the national economy. Support can take a number of forms, including direct subsidies, low-interest loans for production facilities, and governmental absorption of potential losses.

Governmental actions affecting production costs also include regulatory policies—factory environmental standards, worker safety procedures, or production standards.

Distribution

Government programs that support new technological developments politically may require support for the succeeding stages of innovation, including marketing and distribution. It is in the distribution stage that government intervention can be most damaging to free trade. Governments may protect domestic markets through procurement policies or nontariff barriers. They also may attempt to ensure third-country markets through below-market export credits* or political inducements. Such practices fragment international markets, denying the economies of scale that drive the continuing evolution of advanced technologies.

* Any form of financial assistance, direct or indirect, intended to provide financing in whole or in part for a transaction.

The Emerging Market

The latest area for intense competition in advanced technology industries is the Third World's emerging market—the some 113 countries that account for about 40 percent of the world's GNP. Sales to the newly industrializing nations—Brazil, Korea, Mexico, Taiwan, etc.—are a powerful determinant of success in international competition in advanced technologies. The nations or firms that make initial sales to an emerging nation tend to continue as preferred sources. There is concern that competing exporting governments may offer special inducements for commercial sales such as weapons, nuclear technology, export credits, or bilateral agreements favorable to the purchasing nation. The perceived use of such inducements has already provoked bitter conflicts.

Nontariff Barriers and Procurement Policies

Explicit barriers to trade currently are not the major tools for protecting markets. Tariffs for advanced technology trade are quite low among the industrialized countries. Formal quantitative restrictions are ruled out by the General Agreement on Tariffs and Trade (GATT). The "voluntary restraints" and "orderly marketing agreements" through which exporting nations agree to curtail sales in another country are familiar in traditional industries, but are absent in the advanced technology area. Instead, protected markets are created through national procurement policies, through suspension of antitrust enforcement, and through nontariff barriers to imports, such as customs delays and regulations. These barriers can be quite effective. For example, national procurement policies limit trade in telecommunication products between the large European countries, even though the advantages of large-scale production and the costs of duplicative research and development may justify specialization and free trade.[2]

Nontariff barriers may be institutional and attitudinal factors, such as national loyalties inclining nations to support domestic industries, which effectively prevent import of foreign goods.

Imports of foreign goods that compete with domestic products may be ensnared in complex bureaucratic customs procedures, or marketing of products may be blocked by the interlocking control of business. For example, marketing and distribution firms may be owned by or have a special relationship with domestic manufacturing firms and thus refuse to serve foreign suppliers, or local lending institutions may deny financing for foreign product distribution.

Investment barriers, like trade barriers, may take the form either of overt legal restrictions or more subtle pressures. A country may limit foreign direct investment in certain domestic businesses.

In addition, a government may deny foreign-owned firms "national treatment," i.e., the same privileges as domestically based firms, or foreign subsidiaries may be denied access to low-interest loans, excluded from local procurement, or denied the right to participate in collaborative R&D. In many cases, firms investing in countries seek local participation, perhaps at a majority level, to avoid this "second-class" treatment.

There are several other ways in which governments' restrictions on foreign investments may be to the disadvantage of firms attempting import:

- Firms may be unable to invest in necessary complements to advanced technology exports, such as local parts and services facilities.

- "Offset" requirements or "local content" laws may force firms to produce products in-country (occasionally at low volume and high unit cost) as a condition for access to the local market.

- Firms may suffer unfavorable conditions of technology transfer—e.g., licensing at disadvantageous terms—because the preferred route of direct investment is closed.

National Practices—Positive and Negative Consequences

The extent to which our national welfare is interwoven with that of our allies in the fields of science cooperation and advanced technology trade is not generally appreciated. The costs and risks of protectionist policies and market fragmentation are probably greater than in almost any other economic field except energy. Paradoxically, the international coordination of trade practices is more backward in advanced technology than in many other fields at a time when both nations and regions within nations are looking more and more to advanced technology as a primary source of economic salvation.

Innovation proceeds most rapidly and efficiently when new products have access to the widest possible markets, thus spreading the costs and risks of innovation over more units and generating the cash flow for follow-on improvements and further innovation. Thus, the United States should negotiate in international forums to secure the openness of world markets to innovative entrepreneurs wherever they may be based and to eliminate those national actions practiced by other countries that distort the free market operation in the United States. Such a policy is required, both to preserve the U.S. position as a major source of innovation and to ease growing tensions among the industrialized allies, tensions that threaten not only international economic and political management, but also mutually beneficial cooperation in science and technology.

There are a number of practices that effectively close markets in a given country to the advanced technology products of another country. Government intervention to force purchase of products from domestic suppliers is an example. Such practices reduce the total size of the market open to an innovator, reduce the rewards for the innovating firm, and limit the distribution of innovative products globally. Other practices may result in one country's rapidly acquiring a larger share of the market in another country than would occur under conditions of free competition. Export credits on highly concessionary terms is an example. Some practices may not be outlawed by international agreement, but may be injurious to trading partners. An example would be the suspension of antitrust policy for specific advanced technology industries in order to accelerate product innovation and foreign sales.

Commercial and financial practices that are generally agreed to be harmful to the world trading system as a whole, even if at least temporarily advantageous to the perpetrating country, are not necessarily the ones that cause the most damage. While it may be easiest to eliminate by agreement the practices that are acknowledged to be unfair and that add nothing to aggregate world production, it may be more urgent to take aim at some more debatable tactics that cause clear danger. These tactics are difficult to categorize, but they may be the most important and call for the most immediate hard bargaining. They may be protectionist, trade-distorting, or harmful to world welfare. Examples of such practices are:

- Predatory pricing sales abroad at prices below the domestic selling price or below cost. (Below-cost pricing may be defined as pricing that does not permit recovery of production costs over any plausible projection of the learning curve. This may be very hard to define for advanced technology products because of the steepness of the learning curve and because of the subjectivity of business judgments as to how long a time is reasonable for recovery of "front end" costs.) When systematically applied, predatory pricing can be used to "pick off" one sector after another. Protection against this practice is not readily available from either GATT rules or traditional domestic policies of the U.S. government.[3]

- "Targeting" of specific U.S. advanced technology markets by foreign countries through governmentally orchestrated industrial strategies that suspend normal business or regulatory practices with respect to the targeted product line, such as cartelization. Coordinated "picking off" of particular U.S. markets through a concentrated effort is especially pernicious.

- Nontariff-type barriers that effectively exclude U.S. products from fair competition with local products in local markets.

- Government intervention to force purchase of products, especially advanced technology capital goods, from domestic suppliers despite competitive price and/or performance of foreign products. (This would include "Buy American" requirements on U.S. federal or state government contractors.)

- Restrictions on foreign direct investment, particularly those that effectively deny distribution outlets for U.S. advanced technology products in the host country.

- Exclusion of U.S. foreign subsidiaries from "national treatment" equivalent to that afforded national firms.

- Use of political leverage or concessions to influence purchasers in third-country markets to buy a foreign product in competition with a U.S. product. This includes tying sales to trade agreements, military weapons support, nuclear development projects, economic/regional assistance, and similar programs.

- Official or unofficial preferential government procurement favoring domestic producers when contrary to GATT rules.

- Capital or operating subsidies, including concessionary loans that result in extra market penetration of foreign advanced technology products into U.S. markets or world markets. Invocation of the GATT subsidy rule may provide some protection for the injured party. Unfortunately, unless it is vigorously pursued by the firms and country affected within the framework of the GATT rules for subsidies, redress is obtained too late to prevent substantial damage.

- Export credits on highly concessionary terms, based on government subsidies. In the absence of international agreement on what constitutes a reasonable concessionary interest rate, however, it is difficult to fix a criterion unilaterally that would trigger retaliatory action. Such retaliation might be equal or better concessional terms.

- Practices that stimulate innovation by relaxing various domestic rules in the exporting country may nevertheless have some positive spill-over effects. They might be best matched by adopting similar modifications of domestic ground rules for the competing industries in the importing country. If the rule changes were relatively mild—for example, exempting research consortia from antitrust regulations, or permitting patent or other information exchanges among competing domestic firms—the net effect might even be positive.

- R&D subsidies to accelerate the development and commercialization of particular products. Such targeting is considered difficult by many, yet the Japanese record of success seems to be good.

- Exchange of technical information and agreed product specialization (or "market sharing") among competitive firms in a broad technological area. It is frequently pointed out that Japanese law and administrative interpretation permit a degree of both market sharing and technical cooperation in domestic markets that would be illegal under U.S. law and/or regulatory policy. While this may be "unfair practice" from an American point of view, it is within the traditions of the Japanese system.

- Mutual support among independent firms belonging to industrial "groups" whose members enjoy preferential financial and intellectual or other cooperative relationships with each other. Such "group strategy" gives the practitioner a relative competitive advantage in the American market. It represents the kind of rationalization pursued by large U.S. corporations in the early twentieth century that U.S. antitrust policy was designed to prevent. It may be acceptable, however, when viewed from some standpoints, e.g., buyers in the emerging market rather than from the standpoint of "fair competition" with the United States.

U.S. International Negotiating Strategies

In the preceding discussions, we have described governments' practices affecting their respective advanced technology industrial systems and suggested criteria for assessing those actions according to their consequences for the international trading system. These criteria place value on maintaining open markets, thus rewarding innovators, and making innovative products available globally. We believe that the United States must continue to negotiate in international forums to maintain international systems that foster healthy, mutual competition in advanced technology. Such competition will be to the ultimate economic advantage of the world.

The United States must give immediate attention to efforts to strengthen its advanced technology capacity and international trade competitiveness. Such efforts will require both a national focus on the importance of advanced technology to U.S. military and economic interests and the need to compete vigorously in international markets. Recommendations for domestic actions will be discussed in Chapters 3 and 4.

We recognize that there may be circumstances in which, although our domestic advanced technology capacities are well nurtured and strong, still a few key technological sectors essential to our national welfare may be endangered. Successful aggressive policies of our allies could create such vulnerability. If capabilities in a significant advanced technology sector, deemed essential to U.S. economic and military interests, are seriously endangered because of the loss of markets, the United States must take remedial actions. Damage to the nation's total innovative capacity, however, is far more pernicious than adverse impact on a particular product or firm.

A first step is to seek to renegotiate multilaterally agreed rules in forums such as the GATT. Such negotiations should seek to establish clearer guidelines for government actions in high-technology sectors. A basic requirement of such negotiations would be that countries, including the United States, be prepared to consider altering traditional practices.

When there is a specific threat to U.S. interests from a particular country's government policies, the U.S. government should initiate bilateral consultations within the framework of GATT and other appropriate multilateral institutions. The goal of such negotiations would be to reach agreements on a time scale that would prevent or reverse damage to U.S. capacity for technological innovation. If these bilateral consultations are unsuccessful in resolving the issues, the U.S. government should utilize formal multilateral dispute settlement procedures to seek a resolution. If those procedures fail or if the threat of damage is imminent, the United States would be required as a last resort to take unilateral action to protect the national interest.

NOTES

[1] Japan Committee for Economic Development, *Building an Industrial Structure for the 21st Century* (Tokyo: JCED, 1982), pp. 14–15.

[2] Organisation for Economic Co-operation and Development, *Telecommunications Equipment Industry Study* (Paris: OECD, 1981), p. 19.

[3] The negotiations in the Tokyo Round of GATT on subsidies developed criteria for "material injury" caused by such subsidies. Such criteria would probably define the limits of acceptable practice even when a theoretical argument might conclude that the causative practice resulted in a total mutual benefit that exceeded the injury to one of the parties. Certainly in the case of subsidies to advanced technology industries, the machinery of GATT should be available, although the standards of proof of injury may be harder to apply in the case of advanced technology than for other goods. Richard Rivers and John Greenwald, "Subsidies and Countervailing Measures," *Law and Policy in International Business*, 2 (1979), pp. 1465–1495.

THREE

Policies and Practices
Affecting U.S. Competitiveness
in Advanced Technology

THREE conclusions emerge in examining the varying practices of nations toward advanced technology development and trade: (1) other nations do indeed have comprehensive national plans supporting technology and trade objectives; (2) the United States does not take a cohesive and coordinated look at its policies and practices and those of our trading partners regarding advanced technology; and (3) the United States has available to it tools for addressing the needs of its advanced technology enterprise, to strengthen both its capacity for technological innovation and its international trade competitiveness.

Such tools include federal programs for support of research and education; governmental policies and practices with regard to taxes, antitrust, patents, regulation, and technology exports; and broad national economic policies.

Clearly many of these policies and practices are designed to support other national objectives. In the processes of policymaking and allocation of resources, however, the nation's technological capacity and international competitive strength must be highly valued among national objectives. Furthermore, the variables affecting the U.S. advanced technology enterprise must be well understood. This may be accomplished by a high-level assessment reviewing domestic governmental and private actions, the industrial and trade policies of other nations, and the broad global environment. The United States has no adequate assessment process now. In consequence, governmental policies evolve without any broad assessment of how they will affect the strength of U.S. advanced technology capacity and trade.

One reason for this oversight is that the United States views technology and trade policies differently than its competitors do. The United States formulates its trade policy in terms of a process; it sets rules for competition and lets the private sector operate within that framework. Some other countries tend to choose a desired outcome and then define policy accordingly.

Furthermore, the United States views international competition as having rules defining a "level playing field" for firms from different countries—the game should then be left alone. But some other countries, having decided on desired outcomes of the competition in terms of, say, market share or employment, feel the rules allow them to intervene if their national firms are not doing as well as they would like. This difference in approach makes negotiation difficult.

The often adversarial relationships of U.S. government and business, evolved early in the country's history, also may impair U.S. competitiveness. Industry and government have to be prepared to work more cooperatively in order to achieve national goals.

A further problem is that policymakers are rarely people experienced in the industrial innovation process—those who through active experience know the difficulties of creating, producing, and marketing new products and processes embodying advanced technologies. Maintaining a continuing expertise, through a highly qualified and stable government career staff, is a corollary difficulty.

Finally, U.S. companies often see themselves competing against national systems rather than individual foreign companies—U.S. aircraft manufacturers see their competitor as a government-supported consortium; individual semiconductor, robotics, and computer manufacturers here face a cooperative network of Japanese companies working with a governmental agency. So mixed an international trading system complicates international negotiation and agreement.

Government Policies

Macroeconomic Environment

While the depressed worldwide macroeconomic environment intensifies the pressures we have been describing for every nation, the effects may be greater in the United States than elsewhere. Some of the erosion of the U.S. lead in advanced technology may be blamed on macroeconomic factors, particularly the low rate of investment and the consequent slackening of demand for new technologies.

U.S. macroeconomic policies obviously serve a range of national needs beyond those of the advanced technology enterprise, but their impact on U.S. technological development should be well understood. Slack domestic demand reduces the current profits of all firms, their ability to finance investment, and the expected profitability of new investments in capital or technology. The problem is intensified in the advanced technology sector because the payoff to new investments is more uncertain and comes after a longer delay than in traditional industries.

Further, advanced technology industry is unusually vulnerable to high real interest rates that work differentially against long lags in cash flow. The mix of macroeconomic policy in the United States has caused interest rates to be high and volatile for a long time. Apart from the effect already mentioned, this choice has caused the dollar to appreciate substantially against other currencies. The strength of the dollar relative to the yen, especially, makes U.S. firms less competitive precisely in those markets that are endangered for other reasons. Finally, inflation may have inhibited investment in long-range planning and new technology.

Antitrust Policy

While U.S. antitrust policy has begun taking international competition into account, its implementation still fails to give sufficient weight to international trade considerations. The manner in which antitrust statutes are interpreted and applied is charged with interfering in international competitiveness. For example, firms have difficulty retaining the benefits of research that are the product of multifirm collaboration; prospective "safe-harbor" rulings are not readily available; and there is a general uncertainty regarding what corporate actions may elicit legal actions on the basis of antitrust legislation.

Because of this uncertainty, management cites antitrust policy as creating excessive risk for a range of activities that may benefit innovation and trade, such as pooling research efforts, pooling information on the work of international competitors, or pooling development programs whose costs are too large for any one firm in an industry to undertake. By contrast, foreign governments—for example, Japan and France—encourage cooperation among firms through mergers or cooperative programs.

U.S. antitrust policy, however, has successfully fostered beneficial domestic competition. Any changes must be carefully considered. But, in the context of the new era marked by increased relative importance of international trade, by offshore production and investment, by the emergence of world-scale markets, and by the differing policies of other nations, antitrust regulation and enforcement should be reexamined in the light of the international context in which U.S. firms must compete.

Capital Supply

Cost and availability of financing are major factors, both in the start-up and growth of new companies and in the modernization of established firms. Over the past decade, capital costs have been 50 to 100 percent higher in the United States than in Japan.[1] The supply of venture capital for new U.S. firms, however, is large and flexible; that contributes significantly to the abundance of small advanced technology firms here.

Technological innovation by large established firms requires both the capital and the incentive to make large-scale investments. Japan appears to have an advantage over the United States in this area because the cost of capital in Japan (in real terms) is lower due to more thrifty savings habits and superior macroeconomic performance. The difference is aggravated by the economic volatility that has characterized the United States during the last decade. Also, financing of large firms in Japan is less dependent on open capital markets than is true for their American counterparts; thus, Japanese firms' abilities to invest are not dependent on promises of short-term results.

To take one example, Japanese semiconductor firms, some of which are part of large industrial groups that include banks, tend to be heavily financed from within the group.[2] U.S. firms are competing with foreign firms that receive their capital at reduced rates from their governments or from banks encouraged by their governments.

Export Policies

Ideally, we would prefer a world without corruption, without trade restrictions against our allies, without government financial support for exports. We would like to expand U.S. trade in a free-market environment. At the same time, we would like to limit the military technological development of our potential adversaries. However, our pursuit of these objectives must be tempered by our interest in the health of U.S. industry.

U.S. advanced technology firms operate in an increasingly competitive world market. Americans should be conscious of the impact of U.S. policies on U.S. exports as they help or hinder viability of advanced technology firms. This competitive environment need not deter American pursuit of their major objectives, but such pursuit must acknowledge what is realistically attainable and may entail compromises with this reality.

For example, some of our leading competitors justify using official export credits because they protect jobs and nurture industrial development. Until we can achieve agreement to minimize government sponsorship of export credits, we should be prepared to provide similar support for our own industries as we have done in the past through the Export-Import Bank.

Similarly, the United States imposes on exports to currently out-of-favor nations controls for both foreign policy and national security reasons. In the past, these restrictions have been partly based on the questionable assumption that the United States had an effective monopoly in providing the products in question. The consequence may be a loss of U.S. sales; the foreign policy goals may not be achieved. To be in the best interest of the nation, the economic and political costs and benefits of controls must be carefully assessed, and they must be undertaken multilaterally—consulting and cooperating with other leading industrial or agricultural countries.

Tax Policy

Because technological progress diffuses throughout the economy, there is a strong case for special tax treatment for research and development. Indeed, the Economic Recovery Tax Act of 1981 offered several incentives to business investment, including subsidies

47

for a five-year period for research and development expenditures and accelerated write-offs for capital expenditures. The United States is not alone in providing tax incentives for industrial research and development, though many nations prefer to provide direct subsidies. Sometimes new and rapidly growing advanced technology firms are targeted for benefits such as accelerated depreciation and tax benefits during their start-up phases. Policy assessments of the effectiveness of current tax policy in support of research and development (for example, the actual effect of the five-year limit mentioned above) would be welcome.

Regulatory Policy

Health, safety, environmental, and other regulations have been criticized for raising the costs of product development and manufacture, and thus raising prices of American products. The counterargument is that added costs are warranted because of their benefit.

There is now a general mood in this country for reexamination of regulatory policies. That reexamination should include consideration of the effect of regulatory policies on the capacities of U.S. industries to innovate and to compete in world markets.

Private Sector Policies

Nongovernmental variables affecting the advanced technology enterprise may be influenced by government policy. These include the nature of corporate management, university-industry relationships, and financial resources.

Management

American industrial management, long regarded as the standard for excellence, has recently come under criticism. Failure to maintain product quality, searches for short-term market payoffs, and failure to invest in long-term technological innovations are some of the alleged faults. Management has been accused of placing undue emphasis on short-term financial goals, yet our system requires companies to fund their own growth—even and especially in a recessionary period.[3]

Short-term financial concerns have come to dominate many U.S. corporations for various reasons—among them the increased size and complexity of corporate structure, the harsher macroeconomic climate, the uncertainty in government regulation and policy, and (somewhat ironically) the intensifying international competition. Managers equate this near-term emphasis with the need to survive, yet the result—a reluctance to take long-term risks—sacrifices major technological innovations. A blanket indictment of American management is simplistic and erroneous, of course. Examples abound of technologically astute management willing to take risks and invest in an innovative future.

Effective application of American styles of management coupled to a deeper understanding of the critical role of technological innovation in future economic growth may be more appropriate than studying Japanese or other management models. The rapid evolution of advanced technologies offers remarkable opportunities for corporate exploitation and growth. Despite the recession, U.S. industry has seen those opportunities and responded by increasing its research and development spending by 15 percent in 1981.[4]

University-Industry Relations

Historically, the federal government has provided the majority of funds for academic research. Industry has contributed only modestly—4 percent to 6 percent yearly of total academic research and development expenditures from 1960 to 1981.[5]

University-industry collaborations can be, nevertheless, remarkably effective in improving the transfer of advanced technology research results to commercial applications. An obvious example is the influence of MIT and Stanford University in contributing to the growth and success of advanced technology enterprises populating Boston's Route 128 and Palo Alto's Silicon Valley.

New university-industry relationships are emerging in such fields as biotechnology and electronics. Stanford University's Center for Integrated Systems and Carnegie-Mellon University's Robotics Institute have benefited from corporate support in establishing multimillion-dollar research facilities.

We applaud such efforts, and we encourage universities and industry to continue to enter into collaborative arrangements that may

49

create new knowledge, quicken its commercial translation, and strengthen components of the nation's advanced technology capacity. It is crucial, however, that those involved must ensure that research findings in the university are generally open and available to the entire scientific community. Deviations from this rule should be fully disclosed, should be under constant scrutiny and review by the universities and companies themselves, and should be based only on the most compelling short-term reasons. This need not obviate targeted industrial research grants to universities consistent with rewards to the sponsor. In addition, such openness will maintain the concept of free scientific communication and open university.

Government and Private Policies

The following are areas for which both government and private sector actions affect national capabilities.

Human Resources

The U.S. educational system, public and private, is complex. It involves local, state, and federal governance, and its funding sources range from state subventions to indirect cost charges against research. A coherent examination of the educational system within a broader review of policies and practices affecting the nation's technological capacities is not easy, but it is necessary.

A diverse set of human skills is essential to national technological innovative capacity: a technically competent labor force, a first-rate and constantly freshened basic research force, and well-trained baccalaureate and graduate engineers, scientists, and technologically sophisticated managers.

Advanced technologies are powerful tools, but their power is realized only through individual imagination applying them in novel ways. This requires that some technological sophistication be prevalent throughout the population. To illustrate, about half of research and development done in the manufacturing sector flows to the service sector—insurance, banking, utilities, transportation, education, etc.[6] Such flows—and the economic gains they provide—occur because of the technological understanding and imagination of those working in both sectors.

The United States still has the Western world's largest technologically sophisticated population, both absolutely and in the numbers of scientists and engineers as a proportion of the total work force. Since the early 1970s, however, it has been adding to its pool of scientists and engineers more slowly than Japan and West Germany.[7]

Precollege Education

The American primary and secondary high school system for teaching science and mathematics is in trouble. State-by-state statistics show insufficient numbers of qualified science and mathematics teachers. A 1981 survey revealed a shortage of high school chemistry teachers in thirty-eight states, of mathematics teachers in forty-three states, and of physics teachers in forty-two states.[8] American high school graduates have quantitative skills and understanding of science and technology that are today inferior to those of their counterparts in Japan, Germany, and the USSR. The higher productivity growth of the Japanese economy has been attributed, in part, to the high quality of Japanese secondary science and mathematics education.[9]

University Education and Research

The close coupling of research and graduate education is the core of the strength of the American research system. The system is now suffering not only a virtual stasis in research funding, but also squeezes on endowments of private universities and diminished governmental support for state universities.

Total national basic research spending averaged 4.4 percent annual growth from 1975 to 1980, with the federal government accounting for 70 percent of that increase.[10] Growth has tapered off since then and would be negative but for increased research spending in defense and space. The effect on universities of diminished growth in resource funding is direct, given that they accounted for half of all basic research expenditures in 1981 and given that basic research was 69 percent of all academic R&D expenditures.[11] A direct result of this funding lag has been a deterioration in the utility and availability of scientific instrumentation in university research labora-

51

tories. It is estimated that modernizing university equipment alone would cost at least $1 billion.[12]

While the federal government historically has distinguished support of research from support of universities per se—in contrast to the dual-support systems of France, West Germany, and the United Kingdom—that distinction is necessarily somewhat arbitrary in the case of the research universities.

Engineering Education

Problems in training future scientists and engineers are apparent in U.S. engineering education. While Japan, with a population less than one-half that of the United States, graduates more engineers than does the United States,[13] the deeper issue is the quality of education received by American engineering students, both at the baccalaureate and the graduate level. The large number of unfilled engineering faculty positions—estimated in 1980 to be at least 1,800[14]—spells serious trouble for the quality of engineering education, particularly because undergraduate engineering enrollments are at an all-time high. The unfilled positions are commonly attributed to higher salaries in industry than academe. Industry attracts bachelor-degree engineers in ever greater numbers—a process that has been aptly termed "eating our seed corn." And, as with the sciences, university engineering education is beset by deteriorating and obsolescent instrumentation.

Monitoring International Technology

Many nations have developed mechanisms for monitoring foreign technological developments and reporting them back to their domestic industries.[15] Nothing comparable exists in this country. Several facets of the issue might be examined, including any barriers to industrywide collaboration in acquiring and sharing foreign technological intelligence and mechanisms for public and private cooperation in acquiring and disseminating technical information.

Support of Basic Research and Development

We have emphasized earlier the various approaches that the United States and other nations take to the support of research and of various stages of development. The U.S. federal government has accepted its role as the patron of basic research in the United States, and the issue, therefore, is the level of support and the relative emphasis given to various fields.

Support for development, as well as for applied research, is a more difficult matter, involving not only levels of support but even whether support for these endeavors is a federal responsibility. Development is supported in defense, many areas of space technology and aeronautical research, agriculture, and some areas of energy. Some advocate broadening support to include advanced technologies; others oppose this on the grounds that the federal government does poorly in choosing which technologies to support.

What Policies Are Appropriate?

The traditional U.S. position on the government role in supporting advanced technology development and trade has been that governments should restrict their intervention to basic research and education and leave the other components (development, production, distribution, etc.) to the marketplace. Our competitors, however, do not accept this view; they intervene to support the advanced technology system at all stages—research through marketing. The traditional U.S. instruments used to foster technological industrial performance still may be adequate in the face of the more intrusive policies of other countries; but they can be truly effective only with a coordinated and national focus on strengthening the nation's trade competitiveness and advanced technology capacity.

Certainly, any change in the use of existing instruments, or the addition of others, means a major departure in governmental policies toward the industrial economy. However, given the intervention of other governments in international competition, such a departure should be widely debated. For the reasons cited in the first chapter of this report, the United States must maintain the strength of its national capacity for technological innovation. That capacity can be damaged by weak domestic policy. It can also be damaged through practices of our industrialized allies. The problem in responding is to define policies that maintain our technological strength and comport with our national character and values.

53

NOTES

[1] "An Assessment of U.S. Competitiveness," p. 79.

[2] See M. Thérèse Flaherty, "Determinants of Market Share in International Semiconductor Markets," a presentation to the Panel on Advanced Technology Competition and the Industrialized Allies, Washington, D.C., February 9, 1982, pp. 1–13.

[3] Robert J. Hayes and William J. Abernathy, "Managing Our Way to Economic Decline," *Harvard Business Review*, July–August 1980, pp. 67–77.

[4] National Science Foundation, *National Patterns of Science and Technology Resources 1981* (Washington, D.C.: U.S. Government Printing Office, 1981), p. 10.

[5] Ibid., p. 21.

[6] F. M. Scherer, "Research and Development, Patenting, and the Microstructure of Productivity Growth," a report to the National Science Foundation, June 1981.

[7] National Science Board, *Science Indicators 1980*, p. 4.

[8] Paul Hurd, "The State of Precollege Education in Mathematics and Science," presentation to a Convocation on Science and Mathematics in the Schools, National Academy of Sciences, Washington, D.C., 1982.

[9] New York Stock Exchange, Office of Economic Research, *People and Productivity: A Challenge to Corporate America* (New York: New York Stock Exchange, Inc., 1982), pp. 10–13.

[10] Calculated from data on basic research expenditures by source, National Science Board, *Science Indicators 1980*, p. 255.

[11] National Science Foundation, *National Patterns of Science and Technology Resources*, p. 12.

[12] National Research Council, *Revitalizing Laboratory Instrumentation*, the report of a workshop of the Ad Hoc Working Group on Scientific Instrumentation (Washington, D.C.: National Academy Press, 1982), p. 1.

[13] Business-Higher Education Forum, *Engineering Manpower and Education: Foundation for Future Competitiveness* (Washington, D.C.: Business-Higher Education Forum, 1982), p. 13.

[14] John D. Kemper, "Graduate Enrollments in Engineering: Meeting National Needs for Productivity and Innovation" (University of California, Davis, July 1980), p. 7.

[15] For a discussion of some of the mechanisms used by Japan and Western Europe in the field of computer science, see National Research Council, *International Developments in Computer Science* (Washington, D.C.: National Academy Press, 1982).

F O U R

Conclusions and Recommendations

IN this consensus statement, the Panel on Advanced Technology Competition and the Industrialized Allies has described why the United States must elevate, in the scheme of national priorities, efforts to strengthen the nation's capacity for technological innovation, including a vigorous international trade position. The panel believes that the U.S. advanced technology enterprise has been undervalued in the past and now must be placed as one of the nation's most valued objectives. The panel has described also how the United States may negotiate internationally to strengthen the international trading system in harmony with healthy, mutually beneficial trading relations, and how the United States may respond should these international efforts fail.

The following is a summary of the panel's conclusions and recommendations.

Conclusions

- The United States must act now to preserve its basic capacity to develop and use economically advanced technology. This innovative capacity is essential for the self-renewal and well-being of the economy and the nation's military security. Trade in advanced technology products and services will contribute enormously to our economic health. Advanced technology

55

products and processes not only permeate the economy, increasing productivity, but also form the basis of modern defense hardware.

- The nation's capacity for technological innovation is vulnerable both from domestic weaknesses and from damaging practices of other nations. Measures designed to maintain this vital aspect of the American economy within a healthy international trading system will include both domestic actions and international negotiations.

- Effective actions require a sound understanding of the nature of innovative capacity and of the innovation process through which it is primarily manifest. Innovative capacity is the capability, widely diffused throughout the economy, to produce continuously forefront technological resources, and to use those resources for the national benefit. The innovation process includes not only basic research and development, but also production, marketing, and distribution in domestic and foreign markets. Each part of the process must be sound for success.

- Some of the elements that support our nation's innovative capabilities include a strong national research base, technically educated manpower and a technically literate population, capable and farsighted industrial managers, a financial base that provides capital to both new and established firms, and sizable markets. Essential, too, are a national understanding of and attention to advanced technology as a vital contributor to the national welfare.

- The U.S. government has in effect a range of policies and practices including tax policies, patent laws, regulation and deregulation, antitrust measures, export/import bank loans, government procurement, and others that, although designed to serve other national objectives, also affect the U.S. technological enterprise and international trade position. These policies and practices and the other domestic and international elements affecting U.S. technology and trade must be well understood by senior policymakers. If viewed in ensemble, existing government instruments may become powerful means to support U.S. technology and trade interests.

- Responsibility for improving U.S. performance in advanced technology and trade rests to a large degree with the individual firm and its management. Successful managers increasingly will have to be cognizant of frontier technologies as they build businesses and compete in an international world.

- Our major industrialized allies—most notably Japan and France—have designed comprehensive national policies to help ensure successful technology and trade development in major sectors. Thus, individual U.S. firms often find themselves competing internationally, not with firms acting alone, but with countries or with consortia of firms with country backing.

- There is considerable dispute among industrialized allies regarding which practices are acceptable and which are not. Efforts to evaluate practices are protracted and difficult, but essential.

Recommendations

Accordingly, the panel recommends the following:

- Advanced technology development and trade must be considered as among the highest priorities of the nation. These vital interests must be well understood domestically and conveyed to our trading partners. The United States must initiate a two-part strategy: to maintain the nation's capacity for technological innovation and to foster an open healthy international trading system.

- The federal government should initiate a biennial, cabinet-level review that comprehensively assesses U.S. trade competitiveness and the health of the nation's innovative capacity in both relative and absolute terms. This review should consider the nation's overall performance: the private sector activities and the totality of government actions on technology and trade, as well as the effects of other governments' practices. These assessments would consider the strength of key technological sectors across all stages of the innovation process—research, development, manufacture, and distribution. In addition, assessments would evaluate broad elements as they affect innovation, such

57

as the macroeconomic environment, regulatory policy, patent policy, and antitrust policy. Careful attention would be given to maintaining the health and effectiveness of both university- and industry-based research, education, and training. The cabinet-level review should be supported by a continuing mechanism that would draw on expertise both from within the government and from outside.

- Managers of private firms must be cognizant of technological trends as they make renewed efforts to build businesses and compete in an international context. Managers should consider new institutional arrangements—the growing, mutually supportive, industry-university research relationships, cooperative research ventures among groups of firms, or consortia to seek information and ideas systematically from abroad.

- Internationally, the United States should negotiate in existing forums to encourage a healthy mutual trading system. This should include continued efforts to evaluate national trade practices and to agree on criteria for acceptability. An objective must be to encourage open markets and healthy competition.

- Countries, including the United States, throughout negotiations should be prepared to alter fundamental policies so that each country may maintain advanced technology capacities fundamental to its individual welfare.

- The United States should review the content and application of its trade laws to ensure that U.S. industries can obtain timely and meaningful trade and/or other relief in the U.S. market when imports from particular countries, based on unreasonable or excessive foreign industrial policies, threaten them.

- If key technology industries essential to national economic welfare and military security are considered endangered by the actions of another country, even with all necessary domestic efforts to strengthen these sectors, then the United States should negotiate with the other country requesting immediate relief. Negotiations should take place first in existing forums, explaining our country's vital interest in preserving advanced technology capacity. If such mechanisms prove ineffective or too slow to prevent damage to essential U.S. capabilities, then the United States should negotiate directly with the country in question. If those bilateral negotiations fail or if the threat of damage is imminent, the United States should take immediate unilateral actions as a step of last resort.

The panel concludes that the advanced technology enterprise has the potential to contribute significantly to economic and social welfare, both in the United States and throughout the world. It is essential that the industrialized allies work individually and cooperatively toward advanced technology development and a healthy free trade system for their mutual benefit.

Bibliography

Aerospace Industries Association of America, Inc. *The Challenge of Foreign Competition to the U.S. Jet Transport Manufacturing Industry.* An ad hoc study project of the Civil Aviation Advisory Group, Aerospace Technical Council. Washington, D.C.: Aerospace Research Center, 1981.

Baranson, Jack, and Harald B. Malmgren. *Technology and Trade Policy: Issues and an Agenda for Action.* Washington, D.C.: Developing World Industry and Technology, Inc., 1981.

Bergsten, C. Fred. "What to Do About the U.S.–Japan Economic Conflict," *Foreign Affairs,* Summer 1982, pp. 1059–1075.

Caves, Richard E., and Masu Uekusa. *Industrial Organization in Japan.* Washington, D.C.: The Brookings Institution, 1976.

Center for Science and Technology Policy. *Current Issues in Export Controls of Technology: Background Information and Summary of Discussion.* New York: New York University, 1981.

Commission of the European Communities. *The Competitiveness of European Community Industry.* Brussels: Commission of the European Communities, 1982.

———. *Report of the Study Group on Industrial Policies in the Community: State Intervention and Structural Adjustment.* Brussels: Commission of the European Communities, 1981.

Council of Economic Advisers. *Economic Indicators, December 1982.* Prepared for the Joint Economic Committee. Washington, D.C.: U.S. Government Printing Office, 1982.

Defense Science Board. *An Analysis of Export Control of U.S. Technology—A DoD Perspective.* Washington, D.C.: U.S. Government Printing Office, 1976.

de Saint Phalle, Thibaut. *U.S. Productivity and Competitiveness in International Trade.* Significant Issues Series, 2. Washington, D.C.: Center for Strategic and International Studies, 1980.

Diebold, William. *Industrial Policy as an International Issue.* 1980s Project/Council on Foreign Relations, Inc. New York: McGraw-Hill Book Co., 1980.

Elston, C. D. "The Financing of Japanese Industry." *Bank of England Quarterly Bulletin,* December 1981, pp. 510–518.

Forester, Tom, ed. *The Microelectronics Revolution: The Complete Guide to the New Technology and Its Impact on Society.* Cambridge, Mass.: The MIT Press, 1981.

Gray, Paul E. "Technology Transfer at Issue: The Academic Viewpoint." *IEEE Spectrum,* May 1982, pp. 64–68.

Japan–United States Economic Relations Group. *Report of the Japan–United States Economic Relations Group.* Washington, D.C.: U.S. Government Printing Office, 1981.

————. *Supplemental Report of the Japan–United States Economic Relations Group.* Washington, D.C.: U.S. Government Printing Office, 1981.

Kaiser, Karl, Winston Lord, Thierry de Montbrial, and David Watt. *Western Security: What Has Changed? What Should Be Done?* New York: Council on Foreign Relations, Inc., 1981.

Lesson, Kenneth. *Trade Issues in Telecommunications and Information: United States Trade in the Merchandise of Information Industries, 1.* Washington, D.C.: U.S. Department of Commerce, 1981.

Maddox, John. "Science in West Germany." *Nature, 297,* May 1982, pp. 261–297.

Malmgren, Harald B. *Changing Forms of World Competition and World Trade Rules.* Significant Issues Series, 3. Washington, D.C.: Center for Strategic and International Affairs, 1981.

Martin, Jim. "Very-High-Speed Integrated Circuits—Into the Second Generation, Part 1: The Birth of a Program." *Military Electronics/Countermeasures,* December 1981, pp. 52–58, 71–73.

————. "Very-High-Speed Integrated Circuits—Into the Second Generation, Part 2: Entering Phase 1." *Military Electronics/Countermeasures,* January 1982, pp. 60–66.

Ministry of International Trade and Industry. *The Vision of MITI Policies in 1980s.* Tokyo: Ministry of International Trade and Industry, 1980.

National Science Board. *Science Indicators 1980.* Washington, D.C.: U.S. Government Printing Office, 1981.

Organisation for Economic Co-operation and Development. *Impacts of Microelectronics on Productivity and Employment.* Proceedings of a special session of the Working Party on Information, Computer and Communications Policy, November 27–29, 1979. Paris: OECD, 1981.

————. *Industrial Policies for Promising Activities: A Review of Issues, Policies, and Experiences.* Paris: OECD, 1981.

————. *Innovation Policy: Trends and Perspectives.* Paris: OECD, 1982.

————. *International Implications of Government Support Policies for Promising Industrial Activities: Main Issues and Questions for Discussion.* Paris: OECD, 1981.

————. *OECD Economic Outlook, December 1982.* Paris: OECD, 1982.

————. *Science and Technology Policy for the 1980s.* Paris: OECD, 1981.

————. *Technical Change and Economic Policy.* Paris: OECD, 1980.

————. *Telecommunications Equipment Industry Study.* Paris: OECD, 1981.

Reich, Robert B. "Making Industrial Policy." *Foreign Affairs,* Spring 1982, pp. 852–881.

Semiconductor Industry Association. *The High Technology Trade Act of 1982.* Cupertino, Calif.: SIA, 1982.

————. *The International Microelectronics Challenge: The American Response by the Industry, the Universities and the Government.* Cupertino, Calif.: SIA, 1981.

U.S. Congress, Senate. *Reciprocal Trade and Investment Act of 1982* (S 2094). 97th Cong., 2nd sess., 10 April 1982.

————, Senate. *Reciprocal Trade, Services and Investment Act of 1982* (S 2071). 97th Cong., 2nd sess., 4 February 1982.

————, Senate, Committee on Finance. *Trade Agreements Act of 1979* (Report 96-249). 96th Cong., 1st sess., 17 July 1979.

U.S. Department of Commerce. *Advisory Committee on Industrial Innovation, Final Report.* Washington, D.C.: U.S. Department of Commerce, 1981.

————. *Export Control of Technical Data.* Washington, D.C.: U.S. Government Printing Office, 1982.

——. *1982 U.S. Industrial Outlook for 200 Industries with Projections for 1986.* Washington, D.C.: U.S. Government Printing Office, 1982.

Vanderheim, Robert M. "VHSIC: Midterm Report on a Dynamic Circuit Program." *Defense Electronics,* February 1982, pp. 54–62.

Wolf, Nancy L., and David B. Hobbs. *Trade Issues in Telecommunications and Information: The Role of the United States Government in the Financing of Export of Major Telecommunication and Information Products, 4.* Washington, D.C.: U.S. Department of Commerce, 1981.

Wolgate, Robert. "Science in France." *Nature, 296,* March 1982, pp. 285–304.

Selected Reports of the National Academy of Engineering, the National Academy of Sciences, and the National Research Council

National Academy of Engineering. *Antitrust, Uncertainty, and Technological Innovation.* Washington, D.C.: National Academy of Sciences, 1980.

——. *The Impact of Regulation on Industrial Innovation.* Washington, D.C.: National Academy of Sciences, 1979. (Available from National Technical Information Service, Springfield, VA 22161; NTIS Accession No. PB82 116443, Report No. NAE/NRC-OFS-1979.)

——. *The Impact of Tax and Financial Regulatory Policies on Industrial Innovation.* Washington, D.C.: National Academy of Sciences, 1980.

——. *Industrial Innovation and Public Policy Options: Background Papers for a Colloquium.* Washington, D.C.: National Academy of Sciences, 1981.

——. *Industrial Innovation and Public Policy Options: Report of a Colloquium.* Washington, D.C.: National Academy of Sciences, 1980.

——. *The International Technology Transfer Process.* Washington, D.C.: National Academy of Sciences, 1980.

——. *The Process of Technological Innovation.* A symposium sponsored by the National Academy of Sciences, April 24, 1968. Washington, D.C.: National Academy of Sciences, 1969.

——, National Research Council. *The Competitive Status of the U.S. Auto Industry.* Washington, D.C.: National Academy Press, 1982.

————, National Research Council. *The Competitive Status of the U.S. Civil Aviation Manufacturing Industry*. Washington, D.C.: National Academy Press, 1983.

————, National Research Council. *The Competitive Status of the U.S. Electronics Industry*. Washington, D.C.: National Academy Press, 1983.

————, National Research Council. *The Competitive Status of the U.S. Fibers, Textiles, and Apparel Complex*. Washington, D.C.: National Academy Press, 1983.

————, National Research Council. *The Competitive Status of the U.S. Machine Tool Industry*. Washington, D.C.: National Academy Press, 1983.

————, National Research Council. *The Competitive Status of the U.S. Pharmaceutical Industry*. Washington, D.C.: National Academy Press, 1983.

National Academy of Sciences. *Frontiers in Science and Technology: A Selected Outlook*. San Francisco: W. H. Freeman and Co., 1983.

————. *Outlook for Science and Technology: The Next Five Years*. San Francisco: W. H. Freeman and Co., 1982.

————. *Research Briefings 1983: Report of the Research Briefing Panel on Cognitive Science and Artificial Intelligence*. Washington, D.C.: National Academy Press, 1983.

————. *Research Briefings 1983: Report of the Research Briefing Panel on Computers in Design and Manufacturing*. Washington, D.C.: National Academy Press, 1983.

————. *Research Briefings 1983: Report of the Research Briefing Panel on Immunology*. Washington, D.C.: National Academy Press, 1983.

————. *Research Briefings 1983: Report of the Research Briefing Panel on Selected Opportunities in Chemistry*. Washington, D.C.: National Academy Press, 1983.

————. *Research Briefings 1983: Report of the Research Briefing Panel on the Solid Earth Sciences*. Washington, D.C.: National Academy Press, 1983.

————. *Science and Technology: A Five-Year Outlook*. San Francisco: W. H. Freeman and Co., 1979.

————. *Scientific Communication and National Security*. Washington, D.C.: National Academy Press, 1982.

Biographies of the Panel Members

HOWARD W. JOHNSON, *Chairman,* is Chairman of the Corporation of the Massachusetts Institute of Technology. An economist and an authority in management science, Mr. Johnson joined the faculty of MIT in 1955 and was appointed Dean of the Sloan School of Management in 1959. He became President of MIT in 1966 and served in that capacity until 1971, when he was appointed to his current position. Mr. Johnson serves as Director of several major companies and as Director or Trustee of several not-for-profit organizations.

HARVEY BROOKS is Benjamin Pierce Professor of Technology and Public Policy at Harvard University. Dr. Brooks, an educator and physicist, was formerly Dean of Engineering and Applied Physics at Harvard. From 1959 to 1964, he was a member of the President's Science Advisory Committee. Dr. Brooks is a member of the National Academy of Sciences and National Academy of Engineering and a senior member of the Institute of Medicine.

ROBERT A. CHARPIE is President of the Cabot Corporation. Before joining Cabot in 1969, Dr. Charpie was President of the Bell & Howell Company, Chicago. From 1961 to 1968, he served in numerous management positions with the Union Carbide Corporation. Dr. Charpie is a physicist and a member of the National Academy of Engineering.

RICHARD N. COOPER is Maurits C. Boas Professor of International Economics at Harvard University. From 1961 to 1963,

Dr. Cooper was a Senior Staff Economist with the Council on Economic Advisers. He served as Deputy Assistant Secretary of State for International Monetary Affairs from 1965 to 1966 and was Under Secretatry of State for Economic Affairs from 1977 to 1981. Dr. Cooper is a member of the Council on Foreign Relations, and is the author of numerous articles on economic policy.

ROBERT A. FULLER is Corporate Vice President of Johnson & Johnson. Dr. Fuller, a biochemist, joined Johnson & Johnson (Canada) Ltd. in 1955 as a research chemist. He was named Director of Pharmaceutical Research in 1958 and Director of Research and Development in 1961. In 1966, Dr. Fuller was appointed Director of Research and Development for Johnson & Johnson Domestic Operating Company and became Vice Chairman of Johnson & Johnson International in 1975. He was appointed to his current position in 1981. Dr. Fuller is a Fellow of the American Institute of Chemists and a member of the Board of Directors of the Oak Ridge Associated Universities.

RALPH E. GOMORY is Vice President and Director of Research for the IBM Corporation. He is responsible for IBM's research laboratories in Yorktown Heights, N.Y.; San Jose, Calif.; and Zurich, Switzerland. Dr. Gomory joined IBM in 1959 as a research mathematician at Yorktown Heights. In 1964 he was made an IBM Fellow, a rank conferred on a small number of scientists and engineers by IBM. In 1970 he was named Director of Research and was elected a Vice President in 1973. Dr. Gomory is a member of the National Academy of Sciences and National Academy of Engineering. He is a Chairman of the Advisory Council of the Department of Mathematics, Princeton University, and a member of the Advisory Council, School of Engineering, Stanford University.

NORMAN HACKERMAN is President of Rice University. Dr. Hackerman joined the faculty of the University of Texas, Austin, in 1944 and served as Chairman of the Chemistry Department from 1952 to 1961 and President from 1967 to 1970. Dr. Hackerman was Chairman of the National Science Board from 1974 to 1980. He is a member of the National Academy of Sciences and Defense Science Board.

N. BRUCE HANNAY is the retired Vice President for Research and Patents for Bell Laboratories. Trained as a chemist, Dr. Hannay's career with Bell Labs spanned almost four decades. Dr. Hannay has served extensively in an advisory role to academia and the government. He currently is active in board and consulting activities with a number of corporations. Dr. Hannay is a member of the National Academy of Sciences and serves as Foreign Secretary of the National Academy of Engineering.

THEODORE M. HESBURGH has been President of the University of Notre Dame since 1952. Father Hesburgh has served on numerous commissions, including the Civil Rights Commission (1957–72); the Carnegie Commission on the Future of Higher Education; and the Commission on an All-Volunteer Armed Force (1970). He is a Trustee of the Rockefeller Foundation, the Carnegie Foundation for the Advancement of Teaching, and the Woodrow Wilson National Fellowship Foundation and is Chairman with rank of Ambassador to the U.S. delegation, U.N. Conference on Science and Technology for Development. In 1964, he was awarded the Presidential Medal of Freedom.

WILLIAM R. HEWLETT is Chairman of the Executive Committee and co-founder of the Hewlett-Packard Company. From 1969 to 1977 he was President, Chief Executive Officer, and Director of Hewlett-Packard. Mr. Hewlett was a member of the President's Science Advisory Committee from 1966 to 1969 and is currently a Trustee and Chairman of the Carnegie Institution of Washington. He is a member of the National Academy of Sciences and National Academy of Engineering and holds patents on several electronic devices.

WILLIAM N. HUBBARD, JR., is President of The Upjohn Company. Dr. Hubbard received his M.D. degree in 1944 and served as Dean of the University of Michigan Medical School (1959–70) and Professor of Internal Medicine (1964–70) before joining The Upjohn Company in 1970. He was elected President of Upjohn in 1974. Dr. Hubbard is a member of numerous medical honorary societies and currently serves as a consultant to the National Science Board.

SHIRLEY M. HUFSTEDLER is a Partner with the law firm of Hufstedler Miller Carlson & Beardsley. Judge Hufstedler was admitted to the California bar in 1950 and served as Judge, Superior Court, Los Angeles from 1961 to 1966. In 1968, she was appointed Circuit Judge, U.S. Court of Appeals. In 1979, President Carter appointed her as Secretary of the Department of Education. Judge Hufstedler is a Trustee of the California Institute of Technology and the Aspen Institute for Humanistic Studies.

ROBERT S. INGERSOLL served as Deputy Chairman of the Board of Trustees for the University of Chicago from 1976 to 1981, following four years of service with the Department of State, first as U.S. Ambassador to Japan (1972–1973), then as Assistant Secretary for East Asian and Pacific Affairs (1974), and finally Deputy Secretary of State (1974–1976). Before his service in Japan, Mr. Ingersoll spent thirty-three years with the Borg-Warner Corporation. He was Chairman of the Board and Chief Executive Officer of Borg-Warner at the time of his appointment to Japan. In June of 1979, President Carter appointed Mr. Ingersoll Co-Chairman (for the United States) of the Japan–United States Economic Relations Group. Mr. Ingersoll is a member of the Council on Foreign Relations and is Chairman, Japan Society, Inc. (NYC).

CARL KAYSEN is the David W. Skinner Professor of Political Economy and Director of the Program in Science, Technology, & Society at the Massachusetts Institute of Technology. Dr. Kaysen received his Ph.D. in economics in 1954 and was a Senior Fulbright research scholar at the London School of Economics from 1955 to 1956. He served as Deputy Assistant to President Kennedy for National Security from 1961 to 1963. Before joining the faculty at MIT, Dr. Kaysen was Director of the Institute for Advanced Study (1966–76). Dr. Kaysen was also the Vice Chairman and Director of Research for the Sloan Commission on Government and Higher Education from 1977 to 1979.

ALLEN E. PUCKETT is Chairman of the Board and Chief Executive Officer of the Hughes Aircraft Company and has been in key management positions with the company for nearly three decades. Prior to joining Hughes, Dr. Puckett was a research associate in aerodynamics at the California Institute of Technology, Technical Consultant at the U.S. Army Ordnance Aberdeen Proving Ground, and Chief of the Wind Tunnel Section for the California Institute of Technology's Jet Propulsion Laboratory. He has served on numerous industry and government committees, including the Defense Science Board and the Aerospace Industries Association. Dr. Puckett is a member of the National Academy of Sciences and National Academy of Engineering and is the author of several technical papers on high-speed aerodynamics.

DAVID V. RAGONE is President of the Case Western Reserve University. Dr. Ragone was a member of the faculty of the Department of Chemical and Metallurgical Engineering at the University of Michigan, Ann Arbor, from 1953 to 1962. He joined the General Atomic Division of General Dynamics as Chairman of the Metallurgy Department in 1962 and was appointed Assistant Director of the John J. Hopkins Laboratory for Pure and Applied Science in 1965. In 1972, Dr. Ragone returned to the University of Michigan to assume the position of Dean of the College of Engineering. Dr. Ragone is a member of numerous professional engineering societies.

JOHN S. REED is a Vice Chairman of Citibank. Mr. Reed joined Citibank in 1965 and was named Head of the Consumer Services Group in 1974. In 1980, he was appointed Senior Executive Vice President of Citicorp/Citibank and was in charge of the corporation's worldwide banking business with individuals. He was appointed to his present position in 1981. Mr. Reed is a member of the Corporation of the Massachusetts Institute of Technology.

WALTER A. ROSENBLITH is Institute Professor at the Massachusetts Institute of Technology. Professor Rosenblith joined the faculty of MIT in 1951 as an Associate Professor of Communications Biophysics and was appointed Professor in 1957 and Institute Professor in 1975. From 1971 to 1980, he served as Provost of MIT. Professor Rosenblith was a member of the President's Science Advisory Committee from 1961 to 1966. He is a member of the National Academy of Sciences, the National Academy of Engineering, and the Institute of Medicine and currently serves as the Foreign Secretary of the National Academy of Sciences.

ROBERT M. SOLOW is Institute Professor at the Massachusetts Institute of Technology. He joined the faculty of MIT in 1949 and was appointed Professor of Economics in 1958 and Institute Professor in 1973. Dr. Solow was Senior Economist for the Council on Economic Advisers from 1961 to 1962 and a consultant from 1962 to 1968. He has been a member of several presidential commissions and is a member of the National Academy of Sciences.

JOHN E. STEINER is Vice President for Corporate Product Development for The Boeing Company. Since 1941, he has been active in the technology, development, design, testing, certification, product evaluation, and program management of virtually all Boeing airplanes. During his career with Boeing, Mr. Steiner has served in numerous management positions, including Design and Program Head of the initial 727 airplane program (1960–64). He has represented the air transport industry through his many appointments and congressional testimonies in the areas of R&D, industrial productivity, safety, regulations, airline economics, and military procurement. Mr. Steiner is a member of the National Academy of Engineering and the Royal Aeronautical Society of Great Britain.

WILLIAM J. WEISZ is Vice Chairman of the Board and Chief Operating Officer for Motorola, Inc. Mr. Weisz joined Motorola in 1948 following receipt of a degree in electrical engineering. He was elected a Vice President in 1961 and President in 1970, and in 1972 became Chief Operating Officer. In 1980, he was elected Vice Chairman of the Board, continuing as Chief Operating Officer. In 1981, Mr. Weisz was presented with the Electronics Industries Association's highest personal recognition, the Medal of Honor, for his outstanding contributions to the advancement of the electronics industry.

LEONARD WOODCOCK served as Ambassador to China from 1978 to 1981 and Chief of Mission with rank of Ambassador for the U.S. Liaison Office in Peking from 1977 to 1978. Mr. Woodcock was International Vice President of the United Auto Workers from 1955 to 1970. He was elected President of the UAW in 1970 and President Emeritus in 1977.

PART TWO

BACKGROUND PAPERS:
POLICY ISSUES IN
ADVANCED TECHNOLOGY

The papers in this section were selected by the Panel on Advanced Technology Competition and the Industrialized Allies to provide background for its deliberations. They reflect the views of their authors and do not necessarily reflect those of the National Research Council.

International Competition in High-Tech Industries: The Economists' Perspective

Carl Kaysen

THE best contribution that economists can make toward an understanding of international competition in advanced technology industries may be a framework within which to think about it. As a group, we are not particularly good at providing up-to-the minute information. We are about a quarter behind on aggregate economic figures, and usually a year or two behind in detailed knowledge of particular industries. The people operating these industries are always better informed, in detail, about what is going on today. In presenting a conceptual and analytical framework, I will make brief references to past situations, to remind us that some of today's dilemmas are not as new as they appear to be.

The work of the National Research Council's Panel on Advanced Technology Competition and the Industrialized Allies starts from the perception that new technologies—by which I mean a change in the nature of products and the associated production processes—play an increasingly large role in shaping international competition, especially among the advanced industrial countries. The role of new technologies is larger than it was in the past, and it is this new factor that we are concerned with.

Two further propositions lie behind the first. One is that in some respects the pace of technical change itself is faster. The translation process that brings technical possibilities into realization as new production processes or new products is drawing on the stock of new ideas at a more rapid rate. The stock of new ideas is itself growing more rapidly. To be sure, the problem of defining precisely what is meant by technical change or its pace is complicated. Past efforts at sharpening such a definition by giving it a quantitative form have not, in my judgment, been particularly successful. But even if we cannot exactly define technical change, the idea that the pace of technical change is faster than before derives from real characteristics of events in the world of science and technology.

A second background proposition, one less clearly implied by the initial statement of the problem, is that the relationship between technology and economic scale has become different.

It is a familiar concept that some new technologies can be profitably employed only if the market available, either for the products which embody them or for the production processes to which they will be applied, is sufficiently large in scale. Otherwise it will not be worthwhile to make the investment required to use the new technologies. Nathan Rosenberg and others with a historical perspective on economics have studied examples of this principle at work.

A more novel notion holds that there are development decisions that have to be taken on a scale that is now different, and unfamiliar. New technical possibilities seem, more and more, to present all-or-nothing choices and to insist that we must "do it now" or lose the opportunity to do it. Incremental, step-at-a-time decision-making, in this view, may not be able to take advantage of these opportunities.

An example that may be apposite is the decision to develop a breeder reactor with combined government and private funds. Supporters in both the United States and France alleged that some time in the recent past was precisely the time to take the big decision to make a correspondingly big investment in demonstration plants, rather than allowing breeder technology to continue in the mode of research and component development. In that mode the pace would be slower and the process more decentralized, and the government involvement could be less. By contrast, commitment to a precommercial demonstration requires a decision by the government to make an investment or provide a subsidy. The French have made the plunge; we are more than halfway in, but debate still persists on the correctness of the underlying judgment that "now is the time."

Thus we can see novel scale and novel pace in international economic competition, especially the technologically elaborate competition among the market-oriented economies of the industrialized countries—the United States, Canada, Western Europe, and Japan. As we try to understand the consequences of these new features, we have to remind ourselves of the broader context of economic competition in high-technology industries. Two points are worth noting. First, the major international competitors of the United States are also its major political and security allies, as well as its major trading partners. Americans are thus involved in cooperative as well as competitive relationships with our allies, rivals, and trading partners. Anything we do has to be seen in this double light.

A second point to be made is that rapid shifts in the competitive fortunes of particular industries—especially those with large employment and output—are economically costly. They provoke serious political problems in each country of the trading, political, and alliance network within which we operate. For example, the United States and each of its allies found it difficult to say: "Well, the American (or British, or Belgian) steel industry is declining. So be it; the Korean steel industry and the Brazilian steel industry will take its place. This is the way the market is working out, and therefore this is the way things ought to be." It is harder now for any of us to maintain that attitude than it was in the past. The political and economic costs are higher than they once were.

We should also reflect that since the end of the Second World War, the United States has stood for an open international economy. This has been the major continuing thread in our foreign economic policy. We have sought a more open world economy for international investment and capital movements.

However, if we face a distinctly new set of facts, must our policies now be different as well? Should we no longer stand for the most open possible set of rules for trading and investing in the international economy? For guidance, one can look again into the past to examine the dynamics of national positions on the issues of freedom in trade and capital movement. Historically, the stage of development of a country in a particular competitive situation can strongly influence its policies on these topics. Does some historic shift in the U.S. position on these policy questions thus appear likely and justified?

There is a question implicit in the way I have stated the problem so far: is it a real problem, one that is defined—and, for that matter, identified—correctly? One plausible answer is "no." In this view, we are seeing the effects of extra-sluggish cyclical performance, a situation in which for some time inflation was worse in our economy than in the economies of our major trading partners and rivals, and in which, more recently, the dollar has been overvalued. Hence, our troubles in advanced technology trade result from inferior American performance in respect to economic policy both for controlling inflation and for dealing with its consequences. Alternatively (and this is not as plausible), our difficulties could result from a less skillful and less intelligent response in the American economy to the structural shift caused by the large change in energy prices than the responses in the economies of our competitors. Yet we are much less dependent on energy imports than are most of our competitors, and nevertheless it must be admitted that we insulated our energy prices from the world market longer than they did. One can list other, comparable factors that help to account for the generalized poor performance of the American economy and of American economic policy. From this perspective, it would be a mistake to characterize these problems as deriving from a change in the nature and pace of technological change.

This proposition can carry us still further. We start from our traditional belief in an open international economy. We strive for the ideal of uniform treatment by governments of trade, business, and investment, whatever the national domicile of sellers, buyers, and investors. Our international economic policy relies basically on market forces and opens the markets to all. If that is our policy, we must ask ourselves whether a new, special technology policy may simply be a "cover" for a special set of subsidies to a particular group of industries.

Many general public policies do not focus on technology as such, and yet they bear directly on the competitive capacity of a national economy. The design of the tax structure is quite important; so are policies affecting how much individuals invest in their own education. The tax structure is the product of a political market that operates in a quite different way from the economic markets we usually examine. In none of the advanced countries is education viewed solely as a matter of individual as opposed to social investment. It can be argued that a panel considering American technological competitiveness should therefore look at tax and education policies as much as at technology policies.

The current study of American innovative capacity does not require us to answer all the questions I have posed. We do not have to decide whether, by focusing on technology policy, we are misspecifying the problem, and if so, whether we should instead be looking at the broader question of why U.S. economic performance has been sluggish and its comparative standing declining in relation to that of our major trading partners.

I come to this conclusion because it is clear that a strong technological base is sure to be at least part of the answer to our economic difficulties. Many would agree that if there is some generalizable way of improving our technological competence (generalizable in the sense that we are ready to see our trading partners behave in the same way), such improvement will help our economic performance, whether or not failures in American technological performance are a major factor in explaining the bad record. To adapt a Washington cliché, even though the absence of policies to enhance our technological competence may not have been part of the problem, the presence of such policies may be part of the solution. Thus, there is a virtue, independently of how we might answer the earlier questions, in asking whether we can do something to make ourselves technologically more competent.

We also find ourselves partly excused from having to decide whether we are seeing something radically new. Is the pace of change faster? Is the scale on which it is taking place different? Are the decisions that face corporations and governments ones that have to be taken in bigger bites, in larger lumps of capital commitment, or in longer anticipations into the future than was formerly the case? That problem will return when the panel looks at the question of what the United States can do to enhance our technological competence; but I think we can, for the moment, avoid trying to engage it directly.

We are now able to turn to two essential classes of questions. First, what can we do to enhance our general technological competence, to make it easier to generate new ideas and to translate new ideas into new production processes or new products? While there are some areas of production—health care, for example—where business organizations are not the primary producers, for most products and services in international trade competition business organizations are the channel through which new technological possibilities are translated into marketable products and economically useful processes. Second, are there specific industries or specific technologies that deserve particular attention, and on which our efforts to improve technical capabilities should be concentrated? Even though such questions are being restudied by our panel on advanced technology competition, it may be useful to list some of the possible answers, familiar though they may be.

There is some connection—although not a direct one—between the inflow of new ideas into the stock of knowledge and our capability for drawing on the stock to translate knowledge into technical possibility. For instance, understanding more about what the apparently nonfunctioning codons do in a gene will increase in some unpredictable and unknown way, and at some unpredictable and unknown time in the future, the possibility that Upjohn, or Johnson & Johnson, or even Hewlett-Packard will find some way of using that knowledge to make a new product or to provide a new technology for making new and old products. Maintaining or increasing expenditures in support of basic research is one obvious way to make ourselves more capable in basic science and in R&D in general.

We can also make it less costly, in a variety of ways, for the business world to invest in translating technical possibility into reality. Approaches might include direct subsidies of R&D, changing the tax structure, or changing the antitrust rules.

By investing more in education, we could become capable of learning faster and taking earlier advantage of our learning. This applies to the education not only of scientists and engineers—the people who are actually going to produce and apply the new ideas—but also of those who use new ideas at all levels of production and marketing. Such people are important in the process of technical change, so their education is also relevant. Economists, in attempting to dissect the causes of economic growth, to identify and quantify the inputs that result in the output of more product per unit of resources, give great weight to education, as measured by the stock of educated people. Despite the limitations of these measurements, it is hard not to pay some degree of attention to them.

A more specific strategy is to select particular industries—those that have been identified as showing great potential for new technology and rapid growth—and ask what we can do to enhance those potentials.

These are different approaches for responding to what some see as a crisis in American competitiveness in industries that appear to hold the key to our economic future. We will have to decide which track should be emphasized: the general enhancement of capacity for change and growth, or picking important industries and new technologies and specifically helping them to advance. This cursory review of the economists' perspective on technological trade competition can be closed by briefly raising some ancillary questions.

It is sometimes suggested that we should improve our competitive position by holding on to our own technology through the defensive strategy of preventing others from using the new ideas we generate. Such a perspective forces us to examine the question of whether we are spending comparatively too much on basic research.

The United States allegedly spends proportionately more on basic research than most of its competitors and trading partners. Since research findings are published and available to all, foreign competitors applying our results are thought to be getting a free ride. Should we try to prevent them? We might do this by choosing from a spectrum of restrictions ranging from student exchange to access to industrial labs to patent licensing policy.

Alas, results of basic research are particularly hard to hold on to. The whole institutional setting of research is one of openness, widespread conversation, and international collaboration. Representative reports in scientific journals in many of the faster-moving fields of inquiry frequently display the names of four authors from as many different countries. I suspect that an attempt to restrict the "free ride" effect would be unlikely to succeed. But many people, including some in the executive branch and the Congress, are considering such restrictions.

Of course, we could turn the previous question upside down and ask what we can learn from our competitors. What are they doing that we do not do? Americans are already vigorously citing examples, admirable or frightening depending on your perspective, of what other people do that they are not doing.

Most frequently mentioned are the Japanese, but the French and, to some extent, the Germans come in for notice. We point to their policies of directed research, of selection of designated champions, of conscious restructuring of industry in order to make it internationally more competitive. To be sure, it often is difficult to reach reasonable agreement on what is actually happening in those countries; reports vary widely. And then we must ask ourselves whether it is realistic for us to think we can behave like Japanese or Frenchmen or Germans. To describe what they are doing is one thing. But do we have the institutions or the attitudes of mind that permit us to *do* what they are doing?

This important question is frequently neglected. I remember a study of German zoning, city planning, and land use policies that was made some years ago by the Conservation Foundation. The results of these policies are admirable, as almost anyone who visits a German city can see. But the main point of the study was that those policies grew out of a set of institutional and legal arrangements and a set of political structures that we in the United States do not have and will not adopt. No matter how much we want the particular results that we admire, we cannot copy the German methods of achieving them.

Finally, as we consider our response to stiff international competition, we should note that the treatment of research and development in respect to taxes, government subsidies, and the like is an appropriate subject for multilateral rule-making. Thus, it would be a good idea to extend to this area the process of negotiating internationally agreed rules on tariff and nontariff barriers to trade—with more success in the former and less in the latter. The United States should certainly consider the suitability of multilateral rule-making in the research and development area as one method of dealing with the consequences of international competition in the high-technology industries.

Technology Development

Ralph E. Gomory

B ASIC scientific research, with its tradition of open communications in an academic, or academic-like, setting, is widely described and commented on in the public press. Many college graduates have some idea of how scientific research is conducted by
having seen at work the professors who are the backbone of the
scientific professions. The history of science and, more recently,
even the sociology of science are established fields of scholarship.

Technology development, on the other hand, occurs mostly in industrial settings, and many fewer people get to see it. It is usually
not well described in the public press or in the history that people
learn. It is therefore not surprising that the evolution of technology
development is often confused with science in the public mind.

Yet this poorly understood, invisible process of technology development is what we all depend on for improvements in our material
daily life, for the transmission to other countries of knowledge that
we hope will raise their standards of living, and, to a considerable
extent, for our own country's strength and progress.

This article is based on a lecture presented on January 6 and February 5, 1981,
as part of the Charles H. Davis Lecture Series organized by the Naval Studies
Board of the National Research Council. The article was first printed in *Science*,
May 6, 1983, vol. 210, pp. 576–580. Copyright 1983 by the American Association
for the Advancement of Science.

Technological Evolution and Breakthroughs

Technology development is much more evolutionary and much less revolutionary or breakthrough-oriented than most people imagine. It is important to realize that a series of evolutionary steps in technology, together amounting to a large improvement, is just as revolutionary as a breakthrough. That this is the normal course of technology development may be illustrated by two historical examples. These examples are given here not only to illustrate this abstract point but to furnish concrete instances as a basis for a real understanding of technology development.

Steam Engine

The first is the steam engine. The popular notion of the development of the steam engine includes the story of how James Watt was in his mother's kitchen, the kettle boiled, steam came out, and Watt realized the tremendous power of steam and later invented the steam engine. This story has nothing to do with reality, and Watt had nothing to do with kettles. The true origin of the steam engine is very different and much more interesting.

The history of the steam engine may be considered to start in about 1680 with the famous Dutch physicist Christian Huygens, who was trying to develop an engine based on gunpowder. It was recognized at that time that there was power in gunpowder or in fire which, if it could be harnessed, would furnish another source of energy. This could then supplement existing energy sources of the time, which were animal power (for example, horses turning treadmills), wind power (windmills), and water power.

Huygens did not attempt to harness the explosion of gunpowder directly; his method, which was more sophisticated than that, was to explode a little gunpowder in a cylinder, under a piston. The piston was already up, and the idea was that the explosion would create a vacuum and the weight of the atmosphere would then push down the piston. Although it was a rather sophisticated approach it did not work, because the explosion left behind residues and did not create a sufficient vacuum.

However, Denis Papin, an assistant of Huygens, conceived of a way to use steam to create a vacuum. His idea was to boil water over a fire (thus capturing something from fire), put the steam in under the piston, close the bottom of the container, and let the steam cool so that it would condense. This would create a vacuum and down would come the piston. In about 1690 Papin built a model, a small-scale engine of this type, and it worked.

In England, about eight years later, Thomas Savery made the first full-scale working steam engine. He had a number of problems with it. Savery did not use atmospheric pressure. He used steam to drive the piston, and he used it at high pressure. Unfortunately, the mechanical technology of that time was not up to full use of the design. The machine worked but had troubles with high-pressure steam, and its use was restricted by the pressures that the boilers and piping could withstand. It was used mainly for low water lifts to pump water for waterwheels and supply water to large buildings. But this design fell into disuse.

The next step was due to Thomas Newcomen, a plumber. Indeed, one of the morals of this history is that the people who did this work were plumbers, wheelwrights, and instrument makers. Newcomen came up with the first reliable and widely used steam engine. It was basically a blown-up version of the Papin engine. Water was boiled in a boiler and the steam was put into a cylinder. A spray of cold water was applied to the cylinder to cool the steam and create a vacuum, which in turn forced down the cylinder. Then the piston was lifted back up, and the cycle was repeated. The Newcomen engine became important in early eighteenth-century England, where it was used largely for pumping water out of coal mines. This was an important application: many coal mines were unusable unless they were pumped out all the time. In fact, many mines were abandoned because people could not keep the water out. It was a life-and-death problem for the coal miners. The Newcomen engine found a niche where it could survive, and for twenty or thirty years the technology consisted mainly of Newcomen engines pumping water out of coal mines—until it took the next step forward.

Before describing the next step and its effect, a number should be introduced: the "duty," a measure of the goodness and efficiency of engines. This was the number of millions of foot-pounds of work an engine could do by burning one bushel of coal. The duty of the Newcomen engine was about 4. A rough estimate of the work a horse could do for the same cost falls somewhere between 14 and 24.

The next step was taken by John Smeaton, who, around 1767, made a better engine and raised the duty to 7 to 12. Invention, it should be stressed, did not play a major role in this improvement: Smeaton knew how to bore cylinders better. The best mechanics of that time could bore a cylinder for a steam engine only so accurately that one could insert a worn sixpence between the piston and the cylinder. This was why they used the atmospheric engine rather than high-pressure steam—much less steam escaped.

Finally, around 1775, James Watt appeared. The real Watt was an instrument maker, and he got into steam engines because he was given a small model of a Newcomen engine that did not run and was asked to fix it. While working on the problem he realized that energy was being lost by heating the cylinder with steam and then cooling it to condense the steam. Watt solved the problem by supplying the engine with a separate condenser. The cylinder remained hot; the condenser remained cool. This raised the duty of the engine by about another factor of 2.

Later in his life, Watt introduced a two-stroke engine, with the atmosphere driving the piston one way and steam driving it the other. That was worth about another factor of 1.5. The duty was raised by these innovations to between 24 and 35.

In the period 1800 to 1830, engines with more than one cylinder were introduced, and by that time the mechanical technology permitted the use of high-pressure steam. With these innovations, the duty went up by another factor of 2 or 3, from about 37 to nearly 100. The small technology that for twenty or thirty years existed mainly in the business of pumping out coal mines had been transformed, through a series of evolutionary steps, into the energy source that changed the world.

Two points in this story are characteristic of the development of new technologies. One is the cumulative effect of small steps (note that mythological history has erased that and replaced it with a single breakthrough on the part of James Watt); the second is the significance of the niche (in this case coal mines)—the special place in which a technology may survive, even though it is not yet ahead of other technologies of its time in more general applications.

Computer

The second example I would like to discuss is the computer. As a concept, the computer existed in reasonably well-developed form in the first half of the nineteenth century. More than a hundred years ago, Charles Babbage, a well-known English inventor, conceived the idea of a programmable computer. However, the technology of his time—cogs, wheels, and axles—did not permit the easy realization of such an instrument and there was little demand for computation outside astronomical tables. The beautiful idea that Babbage worked out was not realizable in the circumstances of a hundred years ago. It was much later that vacuum tube technology made computers feasible while the impetus for large-scale computing was provided by World War II. The combination of technology and motivation gave rise to the first generation of vacuum tube computers: the ENIAC, EDSAS, and EDVAC, the Whirlwind, the Institute for Advanced Study machine, and many others. There was an early period in which many technologies competed for the role of memory—for example, storage tubes, cores, and thin-film memories. Finally, the transistor, invented at Bell Laboratories, came along and swept the whole development into a totally new phase.

The transistor was a real breakthrough. It was the result of a long buildup of understanding of solid-state physics and then a rather sudden transfer of that knowledge into a new area—the area previously populated by vacuum tubes. Once it got going, this development, like the steam engine, was in the hands of practitioners. It was mentioned before that the evolution of the steam engine was conducted by mechanics, plumbers, and so on. Similarly, the transistor came out of fundamental scientific knowledge, but its continued development was in the hands of semiconductor engineers, where today it is evolving rapidly. In 1968 memory chips held 16 bits, four years later 1,000, and today 64,000 to 128,000. There is every reason to expect 256,000 bits per chip in the next few years, and so on into the indefinite future.

The evolution of the transistor has also spawned the microprocessor, which is often described as a breakthrough, but which can be regarded as such only in the sense of an application breakthrough. The development of the microprocessor was foreseeable. Every year more and more circuitry could be put on a chip. Looking a few years ahead, one could realize that an entire processor, or the central processing part of a computer, could be put onto one chip. Finally it happened, and when it did there was an enormous number of applications for it. That was the main element of surprise.

The arrival of the microprocessor was unavoidable, given the rapid evolutionary progress of transistor technology. I am stressing the evolutionary part, and that is the state that computer technology is in today. I think that the computer is the analogy in our time of the steam engine, in its technical evolution and in its revolutionary impact. If I seem to be down on breakthroughs, it is because I think they are both rare and extremely important. I think we do have them. I do not like to see the confusion that occurs when that name is used for what is just the next step in technology, because it obscures the true nature of much important technical progress that is evolutionary. The transistor itself was a genuine breakthrough. Recombinant DNA and its application to chemical processes are breakthroughs. These are not the next steps in a technology but are the introduction of something quite new.

The transistor was the result of long, patient, and mainly undirected basic scientific work that led to a sufficient understanding of solid-state physics to make it possible. The knowledge that led to its introduction in a field where only vacuum tubes had been before came out of another field. Similarly, the atomic bomb was not the evolutionary outgrowth of explosives but represented the introduction of knowledge about the structure of the nucleus into the field of weaponry. Similarly, recombinant DNA—should it prove to be successful in chemical processing—will be the introduction into a new field of the accumulated knowledge about the fundamentals of molecular biology.

Real breakthroughs do occur; they are rare and stunning events. The more common course of technological evolution is steady, year-to-year improvement, and when that is rapid and persistent, the results are just as revolutionary.

Characteristics of Science and Technology

Armed with these histories of the steam engine and the elements of computer technology, we can raise questions about science and technology. How do they interact? The two examples cited indicate, as many have observed, that it is a two-way street and that science and technology affect each other, and are affected by each other, in more than one way. Of course, we are accustomed to the idea that science contributes to technology. The early history of the transistor is an example of the introduction of scientific knowledge into technology with stunning results. On the other hand, the development of the steam engine was the work of practical men gradually adding improvements driven by the needs of application. This persisted until the 1830s, when the need to make still better steam engines and to understand them stimulated the development of the science of thermodynamics. Technology in that case drove fundamental science. This is happening today; the computer is driving computer science. Furthermore, the evolution of technology makes better scientific instrumentation possible, and this can be a major factor in the advancement of science.

What are some of the characteristics of science and of technology? Science can be thought of as a large pool of knowledge, fed by the steady flow from the tap of basic reesarch. Every now and then the water is dipped out and put to use, but one never knows which part of the water will be needed. This confuses the funding situation for basic science, because usually no specific piece of scientific work can be justified in advance; one cannot know which is going to be decisive. Yet history shows that keeping water flowing into the pool is a very worthwhile enterprise.

Scientific research, which feeds this pool, has its own culture and its own imperatives, which are very different from those of technology. It is motivated by the desire to satisfy curiosity, as opposed to the imperative of technology to get out a working product.

In the United States, science (in contrast to technology) is highly valued. Scientists are esteemed more than the practitioners of technology. Science is primarily university-oriented and to a considerable extent government-funded. The principal citizens of science are Ph.D.s. It is reasonably represented on the national scene. All but one of the Presidents' science advisers of the past (Frank Press, H. Guyford Stever, Edward E. David, Jr., Donald F. Hornig, George Kistiakowsky, and Jerome B. Wiesner) come from the world of science but represent both science and technology. The current relative prestige of science and technology is peculiarly American. The

87

situation varies a great deal from country to country, and in some countries it is considerably different from that in the United States.

Technology is different. It is manned primarily by engineers, not Ph.D.s. It is usually industry-oriented rather than university-oriented. It is driven by applications and products rather than by the imperatives of science. However, perhaps the most important point about technology is that it tends to be very complex.

Because of its complexity, developments in technology are sometimes hard to predict. The problems and the advantages of evolving new technologies are often not obvious. In the early days of the transistor, germanium was selected as a transistor material because it allows electrons to move more rapidly than they do in silicon. This seemed to promise much higher speed. But, in fact, it turned out that silicon almost completely supplanted germanium because it naturally grew on its surface a layer of oxide that protected the finished chip. That practical consideration far outweighed the apparent advantage of germanium. Today we have almost entirely silicon technology.

Another example is Josephson technology, a proposed new computer technology, which relies on superconductivity and some variations on it that occur only in certain metals and at temperatures near absolute zero. We understand all these complex phenomena, but they are not the problems with this new technology. The actual problems are more mundane, but much harder and of the following sort.

The computer itself is complicated. Large computers have to be repaired during their lifetime, partly because things break down and partly because they were designed wrong in the first place (no one has yet designed a large computer completely right). In the course of its lifetime, a large computer has to have the capability of being repaired, let us say 300 times. If you were repairing one of the machines that depends on superconductivity, you would have to take the cooled elements out of their cooling bath to fix them 300 times—and that means that all of those elements would have to be able to withstand the expansion of coming up to room temperature and being cooled off again 300 times without anything going wrong.

The phrase "without anything going wrong" masks another level of complexity. The computer might have 7 million basic elements. Those 7 million elements would all have to be warmed to room temperature and cooled again 300 times with a minimum of failures.

If one failure occurred every time the computer was warmed, then after cooling the computer would have to be warmed up again right away to repair that one failure, which would probably cause another failure, and the result would be a totally inoperative machine. The difficulties in this technology, therefore, are not really in understanding the difficult phenomena; they are in making very tiny elements that can expand and contract 300 times and in creating an assemblage of 7 million of those elements that will almost never have even one thing go wrong with it.

In addition, a machine like a computer has to be manufacturable, and this introduces a whole new set of extremely difficult requirements before all of the small components will work.

To illustrate the requirements related to manufacturability, I will discuss the magnetic bubble device, in which a small thing called a "bubble" moves from one tiny piece of metal to another. For the device to work, the two pieces of metal have to be the right distance apart, or the bubble will not jump the gap. The bubble has to travel within a layer of material (garnet) that must be the right thickness, and it is moved by a magnetic field that provides a particular force. The practical problem is to manufacture these tiny devices with such precision. The two pieces of metal are never exactly the same distance apart; they may be 10 or 15 percent off. The thickness of the layers may vary by 5 percent; the magnetic field is never completely uniform. The result is that the design must have a tolerance window that will permit the device to work even though the distance is 15 percent off, the thickness is 5 percent off, and the magnetic field may be 8 percent off. In addition, all of these things vary with temperature, so that the design also has to take into account a certain temperature range.

In new technology development, even if you are looking at a working device, you may be looking at something that needs a couple of years of redesign work before it is manufacturable, because it has to be designed so it can withstand all those changes and still work.

Cultural Factors

In dealing with technology, things are sufficiently complex that much is done by rule of thumb and not by precise knowledge. Many

89

factors enter in; some of them are even cultural. (I am using the word culture here only to indicate a general set of habits of a group of people. There is no implication that this culture is unchangeable; in fact, it is very changeable.) Let us consider an example. A complex part was being made. It went through a large number of process steps. Only about 6 percent of the parts that came out at the end worked. That was not nearly enough because, with the cost of the whole process, a 6 percent yield made the parts too expensive. On the other hand, no one could find anything seriously wrong with the process. So the engineers moved in and stood where the production people had been, and they carried out the process in the hope of finding out where it was going wrong. They never found anything wrong with it because they got a yield of approximately 60 percent when they did exactly the same thing. Eventually it became clear that the people who had been doing the processing simply had not been trained to be precise enough. Sometimes they put a screwdriver in a hole that was later used for precise positioning. In handling a part they sometimes made little nicks and scratches on it or touched it with their hands. Later, things would not adhere to the surface that had been touched. The accumulated effect of those things made the difference between 6 and 60 percent.

Technology is culture-dependent in other ways. Cultural factors such as attitudes toward financing (long-term versus short-term goals), attitudes toward carelessness and small mistakes (quality), and the presence or absence of the famous NIH (not invented here) syndrome (it is hard to get someone else's idea into your laboratory) have a tremendous influence on technological progress.

The best example of culture interacting with technology is, of course, Japan. I refer not to modern Japan, but to the Japan that was opened up to the world by Commodore Perry in 1854. By 1905 that same country possessed a large textile industry and a manufacturing capability that extended to such complex objects as torpedoes and quick-firing guns. The ability to use the most advanced techniques was demonstrated when the wireless-equipped Japanese fleet defeated the Russians in the battle of Tsushima. Marconi's invention played a key role in this victory, which was its first use in naval warfare. This remarkable transformation from a feudal state to one that was at home with the most technically advanced machines of its time in a span of fifty years is, to my knowledge, unparalleled in the history of technology. That culture has continued, and Japan is once again making tremendous strides. Other countries, for reasons we do not really understand, have had much more trouble assimilating technology. China, for example, which many people consider to have been culturally superior to Japan for thousands of years, has never under any kind of regime been able to make that kind of technological progress. Great Britain, which started and led the industrial revolution, is today strong in science but weak in technology. There is no simple connection between scientific mastery and technological leadership. When the United States and Japan are compared on a scientific level, the United States is well ahead. But on a technological level, it is quite another story.

Technology Transfer

This picture of technology as a complex and even culture-dependent process bears on a number of things, including security, in the sense of secrets, and technology transfer, in the sense of trying to get a technology to someone else in the same country or in other countries.

It is hard to keep a simple idea secret. The idea, for example, of having a separate condenser for a steam engine can be expressed in one sentence. It is hard to keep that one sentence a secret. On the other hand, it is hard to transfer the full complexity of a technology. There is too much. Those who are not technologists in the same field cannot even be sure which details matter. So simple things are hard to keep secret, and complex things like technology are hard to give away.

Let me add a caveat, which is that everything depends on the receptor to whom the secret or the technology is to be given. If the receptor knows very little, he can do very little even with the simple idea, because he cannot generate the mass of detail that is required to put it into execution. On the other hand, if he knows a great deal and is capable of generating the necessary details, then from just a few sentences or pieces of technology he will fill in all the rest. That is why it is hard to transfer technology to the Third World and very hard not to transfer it to Japan.

Technology, more than science, moves forward in a world in which

91

time and expense are extremely important. An experienced colleague of mine, Robert Henle, told me that there is a saying that in technology you never run out of ideas, just out of time. I saw that borne out some time ago when we were trying to get a new printing technology ready. It took longer and longer, and finally we stopped the effort and substituted a conventional technology in order to get the product out. People working on the new technology said that they still had a lot of ideas about how to fix it, and that was true. We had not run out of ideas, but we had run out of time.

New technologies are generally expensive because they are not yet refined. Therefore they often cannot compete with existing, in-place technology, which has been refined. That is where, in the case of the steam engine, the coal mines came in. Often new technologies depend on finding some small use that can keep them in existence while they improve. If they do not find it, they will never reach their full potential, because no one will spend the money to keep them going.

This, incidentally, is an important role that military procurement fulfills, even though it is a small part of the commercial marketplace, because military requirements often place extreme demands on quality and capability that can only be met by new technologies. Those technologies are thus kept going and are given a chance to grow to maturity.

Scientific Knowledge

All kinds of fundamental issues arise in the course of technology development which require the most advanced scientific knowledge or even new scientific knowledge for their solution. The effect of cosmic rays on computer memory is an example. To understand what happens and to prevent loss of information from the memory requires knowledge of the detailed interaction of these particles from outer space with the crystalline matter of the transistors and the ability to trace the effects of this interaction into the memory. So we need directed basic research—that is, work done at the most fundamental level, but intended to get certain practical problems solved. This should not be confused with the important pool-filling activity alluded to earlier.

Organizational Problems

Bringing scientific knowledge to bear on technology is not easy. Inventions or solutions to problems occur when the knowledge of a need and the technical or scientific knowledge to cope with that need finally come together in one head. Everything else is just a means to that end. Those means often become elaborate, except in a very small organization.

Small organizations have their own problems. They usually do not have the technical skill to solve fundamental problems unless they are set up specifically for that purpose. In most large organizations there is an elaborate apparatus that, in one way or another, tries to take knowledge of a need and translate it into a clear-cut technical or scientific problem. The need for more speed in computers in the marketplace may be translated into saying to a person with a knowledge of ceramics, "I need a new ceramic with a lower dielectric constant." This long process of translation usually calls for some organizational apparatus. However, organizations tend to develop a life of their own. The individuals or small groups whose scientific knowledge you rely on and to whom you try to translate your needs may be more interested in ceramic science than they are in computers. The fact that your requirements are written down does not remove the difficulty. Written documents are often worse, because without a dialog between individuals it is difficult to convey exactly what is meant and what is really important. These problems are not easily dealt with. In fact, it is hard to overestimate the diluting and distorting effects of long chains in organizations, long chains of command, or long chains of information transmission.

One way of overcoming these effects is to have people move around. Researchers should know what development is like; developers should know what their product is used for. In that way, these difficulties can be short-circuited to some extent. Another stratagem is now and then to talk to someone at the bottom of the organization and get an exact and detailed account of what he is doing. An executive may think, for example, that his organization is investing in navigation, only to learn that it is investigating turtles laying eggs. That may sound funny, but there is a real connection.

One way to study navigation is to study animals that exhibit remarkable navigational ability. An example is the sea turtle. It is difficult to study sea turtles in the water, so people start by studying sea turtles on the shore when they come out to lay their eggs. That may well be what is going on in the organization, and it may be necessary to decide between producing a new navigational device in a few years or contributing to the basic pool of scientific knowledge, which experience has shown to be useful in the long run.

The usual problems of an organization are made more acute when it is technologically oriented. In an average organization, usually a hierarchical one, there is an implicit assumption that the people with the power to decide, the people in certain positions of the hierarchy, also have the knowledge to decide. In a sales organization, for example, the veteran salesman has first been a sales manager; he knows how to run a branch office, then he runs a group of branch offices, then he runs a region, and so on. He understands reasonably well what it is all about.

In a technological organization, it is often the case that the person with the power to decide does not have the detailed technological information needed to make a decision. These complications can be dealt with. A special task force is often formed at this point. This is an ad hoc group of trusted people with the technical knowledge to investigate the question at the right level of detail and report their reasoning and conclusions to the person in charge.

Morale and attitudes are also important in dealing with this difficulty. Key technical people must feel free to make their views known. The person in charge should also have key technical people, not usually those who report directly to him, whom he feels free to consult. All this is easier in an organization with enthusiasm and a shared sense of purpose and direction.

Conclusion

In this article I have attempted to bring out the evolutionary character and the complexity of much technological development. Technology development is sensitive to detail and to the culture in which it is embedded. It is an activity that is not well understood today, yet we must go forward with it. Much of our individual and national welfare depends on the success we make of it.

Industrial Policies:
How Effective Are They?

Richard R. Nelson

THE Panel on Advanced Technology Competition and the Industrial Allies is concerned with national policies designed to promote high-technology industries and with the international ramifications of such policies. Before examining these issues, it may be instructive to place the current situation in historical perspective. Following that, a discussion of the apparent aims of national policies in support of high-technology industries, and the instruments used to pursue these ends, will lead to a consideration of the effectiveness of these policies in achieving their purposes. It will be noted that industry-specific policies have demonstrated a capability to create or preserve a national industry, if perhaps at considerable cost, even if the nation is not at the technological forefront generally. However, it is questionable whether sustained leadership in high-technology industries can be achieved by narrowly focused policies. Finally, we will turn to some implications for U.S. policy.

A Historical Perspective

Discussion of the efficacy of government in "picking winners" goes back at least as far as Adam Smith. The following lines are found in *The Wealth of Nations* soon after the famous "hidden hand" passage: "The statesman who would attempt to direct private people in what manner they ought to employ their capitals, would

95

not only load himself with the most unnecessary attention, but assume an authority which could be trusted, not only in no single person, but to no counsel or senate whatever, and which would nowhere be so dangerous as in the hands of a man who had folly and presumption enough to fancy himself fit to exercise it." Here Smith is arguing the perniciousness of the import restrictions, special export advantages, and "bounties" in support of domestic industry, prominent on the Continent at that time, which he feared British statesmen might mimic.

Smith's advocacy of laissez-faire took hold in England and later in the United States. However, we Americans ought to recognize that free trade became our creed only after our manufacturing industry was well established and in the technological forefront in many areas. Even during the twentieth century we have sought to nourish and spur the growth of industries believed to be at the technological cutting edge. Consider, for example, our policies during the 1920s and 1930s to foster the development of our aircraft industry. In the postwar era, the achievement of leading semiconductor and computer capabilities has been viewed as an important national security objective and consequently has been fostered by a number of policy mechanisms.

Countries that consider themselves economically or technologically backward seldom have gone along with the prescription that the government's role should be passive. Alexander Gershenkron, in his *Economic Development in Historical Perspective*, has proposed that the more relatively backward a country at the time rapid development commences, the greater the entrepreneurial role played by the state or statelike institutions. There is no question that the governments of late-nineteenth-century Germany, Italy, and Russia were concerned with the perceived lagging positions of their nations and actively encouraged the growth of the "high-technology" industries of that era. Soon after the Meiji restoration, the Japanese government also took on a strong and effective entrepreneurial role in establishing the steel and armaments industries in Japan.

Today, as in earlier times, countries that lag behind technologically attempt to catch up through a variety of policies. The countries in the forefront tend to espouse free trade, while those behind doubt that they will be able to catch up without giving assistance to their industry. This panel is, of course, focusing upon recent national policies in support of industries like semiconductors, computers, telecommunications, and aircraft. To understand these policies, however, I think it helps to recognize them as akin to policies of earlier eras.

Objectives and Policies

Today, as earlier, the stakes that nations believe they are playing for in the pursuit of strength in high-technology industries are diverse and often involve a measure of faith or fear. Almost always there has been a concern with national independence and security broadly defined. In some cases the perceived threat, or objective, has been specifically military. It is no accident that nations defeated in war or frustrated in diplomacy often have responded with aggressive "industrial policies." While often involving an expressly military component, independence and security have usually been construed more broadly as including the ability of a country to chart its own domestic course and not to be critically dependent, either economically or technologically, on foreign powers. In this context, among relatively advanced nations high technology often is viewed as being like a critical raw material. A self-respecting nation should have assured access to it and, where possible, home control. Often operating behind the scenes is a Hirschman-like theory of linkages: nations with strong high-technology industries will grow and prosper generally; those without them are doomed to the economic backwaters, are dependent upon other nations economically as well as militarily, and are treated accordingly.

Concern about technological backwardness and dependency frequently has led to broad-gauged policies to strengthen the nation's general system of scientific and technological structure; this usually involves support of basic research and education and the building of new institutions. Such policies have typically been modeled on those of the perceived technological and economic leader. They may be concentrated on certain scientific and technological fields, but usually are not tightly targeted at specific industries. Another broadly aimed policy is to facilitate effective manufacturing investment through actions that induce high national saving rates and that facilitate the flow of capital to firms in technologically progressive industries.

National strategies to catch up or stay in front technologically usually have also involved a mix of policies targeted at specific industries. Home firms may be given special advantages in the domestic market through a system of tariffs and quantitative restrictions. Defense and other government procurement may favor the home industry. Special access to subsidized capital often is part of the package. In recent years, so also has been industry-targeted R&D funding or subsidy. It is these more narrowly targeted governmental actions that nowadays tend to be called industrial policies.

It appears that the central objective of policies that create or maintain domestic high-technology industries is not commercial profitability in a narrow sense, but rather independence and security broadly defined. This is obviously so for nations concerned about their military strength, such as France or the United States. Indeed, when the countries involved have a large defense budget it is hard to distinguish between defense policies—involving procurement and associated R&D support and investment in plant and equipment— and targeted industrial policies. The United States long has had a policy of "buy American" for most of its own procurement. Even Sweden, a country that, until recently at any rate, has not been accused of specific policies to advantage high-technology industries for economic purposes, has chosen to maintain a Swedish aircraft industry.

The United States has not needed, until now at least, an explicit industrial policy toward aircraft, computers, and semiconductors, because its general and defense policies have sufficed to keep these industries on the frontier. But let us assume for the moment some (unlikely) arms limitation agreement which halted the procurement of all new military aircraft and missile systems but which did not achieve full trust. Assume, too, that in the new regime, where all sales were commercial, companies in other countries were capturing the lion's share of the market, and American companies producing aircraft were apparently about to go out of business. Does anyone believe for a second that we would not adopt an "industrial policy"?

For countries like Japan and the Federal Republic of Germany, security is defined in terms of economic, not military, strength. For both, exports are an important objective in themselves. In that sense, economic benefits account for a larger share of the numerator in the benefit/cost calculation than in the United States or France. But the benefits are seen in terms of general industrial strength, and as diffusing widely across German and Japanese economy and society, rather than being localized in returns to the particular high-technology industries. The objective is to develop, protect, and advance a set of core industries believed to be the key to future economic prosperity and without which a country is believed doomed to being second class, in a political as well as economic sense. From this point of view, it is worth paying a price for national control, so that key decisions affecting the fate of the country are made by nationals instead of foreign corporate managers.

Consequently, even in cases where national defense, in the narrow sense, is not a serious consideration, it is misleading to think of industrial policies as aiming solely for commercial profitability. Of course, if the industries themselves are commercially viable, the needed public investments in them are less and such policies are easier to support. If the price becomes high enough, as in the supersonic transport projects in both the United States and Europe, governments may act to cut losses. But neither in the United States nor in Europe was the supersonic transport project viewed as a strictly commercial transaction. On both sides of the Atlantic the SST project was considered to be a means of supporting the aircraft industry. Thus, in a general sense, industrial policies toward high-technology industries must be understood as involving a strategic conception overlaid by commercial constraints.

Can Narrow Industrial Policies Succeed?

Obviously the answer to that question depends on what one means by "succeed." Can they succeed in establishing and securing a domestic industry, perhaps at continuing cost? They can and they have, although in many cases the continuing cost has been considerable, both in terms of direct government outlays and in terms of the indirect domestic political costs associated with protection. France has preserved its aircraft, computer, and semiconductor industries. Sweden has an aircraft industry.

Can narrow industrial policies help achieve industries which, in due course, can compete internationally in commercial markets without large and continuing direct or indirect subsidies? Again, the answer is that they can and they have, although the initial investments may be considerable and success in this sense is more problematic. Germany, for example, has by this means achieved a formidable capability in certain areas of electronics. On the other hand, despite a variety of efforts on the part of their governments, the French and British electronic industries still look generally weak, and absent protection or subsidy they would probably be in serious trouble. I would argue that the difference between the successful and unsuccessful cases here may have less to do with the nature of the particular focused industrial policies than with the general technological and industrial strength of the individual countries.

Given basic general strength, industry-specific policies can provide the needed extra support, or thrust, to help domestic firms compete commercially on international markets. Examination of the limited case study evidence leads me to conclude that the industry-specific policies which succeed in providing that extra thrust do not, in general, involve massive government support of particular R&D projects. Rather, they involve a more diversified and durable program of building up the technological capabilities of the companies in the industry so that they can place their own bets and win on them.

Can industrial policies lead to industries that are technologically and economically in the forefront in a durable way? My reading of economic and technological history suggests that the *general* industrial policies of a country—the quantity and quality of its support of scientific and technological education, of basic and generic research, the general climate of incentives for investment and the supply of capital—make a considerable difference. Technological and commercial leadership in the high-technology industries of an era will go to countries where the basic conditions are strong. Given that these underlying conditions are strong, industry-specific policies can provide some supplementary assistance. Absent underlying scientific, technological, and economic strength, industry-specific policies can preserve domestic capabilities near the technological cutting edge, but only at considerable cost; and they have virtually no chance of pushing domestic firms into the forefront.

Consider the major success stories. It is clear enough that in the postwar era, policies associated with military procurement gave special help to the American aircraft, computer, and semiconductor industries, and that American firms gained and have held technological and commercial primacy. I argued earlier that in the American case, defense procurement-related policies should be recognized as having much in common with what are called industrial policies in other countries. These cases, then, look like examples of "successes" of industrial policies in the third sense described above. But note that for at least a quarter of a century after World War II, American industry was on the technological forefront virtually across the board. Other countries looked with envy at our general system of scientific and technical education and research support. The overall strength of our technology base and our economy was then unsurpassed. Japan appears to have become highly competitive in the semiconductor field. Certain parts of the computer industry in Germany also look like success stories. But, again, the economies of Japan and Germany have been generally successful, and their rising across-the-board technological strength has been noted by many observers.

Conversely, in the postwar period England has tried to preserve a commercial capability in aircraft and to build one in computers and, now, in semiconductors. She has not been successful. But many observers have commented that England is generally weak in technology and management and has been falling off in these areas, relative to other countries, since World War I.

Let me put my conjecture more generally. Countries that are generally strong scientifically, technologically, and industrially will be those that effectively find, invent, and develop the high-technology industries of their era. When the importance of these new industries becomes widely perceived, their governments may develop specific policies to facilitate their advance. Thus, in a sense the industrial policies are drawn by technological leadership, rather than the other way around. In contrast, where industrial policies aimed at specific industries are put in the forefront and in effect lead, this is because those industries are lagging in that country, and the objective is to diminish the lag.

Industrial Viability vs. Leadership

Narrow-based industrial policies are essentially defensive. A reserved home market can shelter, but in itself provides no stimulus for the home industry to get to the frontier and beyond. Indeed, unless internal pluralism and competition are actively encouraged, as has been the case in Japan, the result of protection may be an industry that can survive only in a hothouse.

Defense and other government procurement has the potential of pulling the capabilities of the home industry to the forefront. However, if the existing capabilities are weak, it is risky to ask that the industry produce what no one has ever produced before. It is safer to ask that it produce what the industrial leaders have already produced. This seems to characterize French and British military procurement strategies. However, by the time the home industry has achieved what the leaders have achieved, the leaders have moved on. Such a policy can pull the domestic industry toward the frontiers, but unless very great risks are taken, it is unlikely to thrust the industry into technological leadership.

I submit that the same situation obtains regarding government-subsidized R&D projects aimed at creating particular new products or processes for a commercial market—what has been called "picking winners." If a domestic industry is technologically lagging, it is highly chancy to try in one leap to go beyond the current frontiers. It is better to be less ambitious. My reading of the scattered history of government-subsidized commercial R&D ventures shows a mixture of ambitious efforts that failed technologically, and more modest efforts that were derivative and not innovative.

Almost invariably, a key component of government policies in support of high-technology industries has been finance of directed basic research and of work on the generic aspects of the technology—that is, support of research aimed at increasing the applied research, development, and design capabilities of the firms in the industry but not targeted at particular designs. The intent is to build up the general technological strength of domestic industry. However, the results of basic and generic research tend to become "public" quite soon. They are hard to keep bottled up for domestic use only.

Many years ago, corporations were more dependent upon access to local scientific expertise, and less tied into the international scientific and technological community, than they are today. Also, companies were much more "national" then, as opposed to international. Today it is not clear that physical proximity to the locus of discovery, or common citizenship, gives a company strong advantages in learning about new scientific developments. When the U.S. government supports basic research at universities, or even in corporate laboratories, strong forces militate against blocking the access of foreign companies to what is learned (unless there is a national security cover). I have not seen much written on the European or Japanese programs in support of directed basic research. It would be interesting to explore the mechanisms, if any, used to block foreign access. If, as I would conjecture, it is difficult to block access, then the benefits of such programs will flow to those companies which have the technological and managerial strength to make use of research results, no matter their nationality.

In the contemporary world, in which many of the corporations engaged in high-technology development are multinational, it is no longer clear what the words "foreign" and "domestic" actually denote. For example, the French provide subsidies to companies located in France but with home offices in the Netherlands, or the United States. French and Japanese companies buy plants in the United States, in part to gain physical and social proximity to the knowledge found in the Silicon Valley. Japan has been more effective than the other major industrial powers in keeping out foreign producers, but one wonders how much longer the dikes will hold.

In a world where information flows rapidly and widely, the advantage goes to those companies in the best positions to anticipate new developments and to seize new opportunities quickly. In industries where the technology is multifaceted and rapidly changing, innovative strength requires the ability to comprehend and deal with constraints and developments across a wide front. It is very difficult to predict in advance where the new opportunities will open up. Sometimes it is process equipment suppliers who are making the major advances, and the product designers must be quick to understand what new design possibilities and requirements are thereby being opened. Sometimes the design is advancing rapidly, and new processes are needed that will accommodate these new designs. Sometimes the key advances are in materials.

A wide variety of firms are thus involved in advancing the technology, in interaction with each other. In rapidly advancing technology, being at the forefront requires exploring a variety of approaches—pluralism, and not a centralized attempt to "pick winners." Even in a nation whose companies generally are at the forefront, some companies in a given industry will be lagging as others are leading; turnover of leadership is to be expected. A variety of scientific and technical skills and knowledge are involved, and the key manpower needs change over time. The companies in the United States, West Germany, and now Japan are powerful in high-technology industries. I would argue that this is a result not so much of narrow government policies which support and stimulate those particular industries, but rather of broad-gauge scientific, technological, and industrial strength.

What Should Our Concerns Be?

If my diagnosis is close to the mark, it may be difficult to talk the trilateral nations out of their policies in support of high-technology industries. On the other hand, the dangers to the United States may be less grave than is sometimes argued nowadays. Indeed, I would argue that perhaps our greatest danger would be to misinterpret the situation and adopt national policies that cannot help us very much, while letting down on the policies that are the real source of our strength.

I doubt very seriously that countries like Great Britain, the Federal Republic of Germany, France, and Japan are going to be easily persuaded that there is not much need for them to have a national presence in the computer industry, the semiconductor industry, etc. Those countries with major defense programs will continue to try to favor domestic companies. Telecommunications procurement will be similarly employed. There is room for some progress in opening up procurement. I suspect, however, that what will be involved here is horse trading.

There is probably more room for bargaining about reducing general home market protection. Certainly this ought to be explored. However, many of the governments are presently taking the stance that they are doing little to protect the home market. In a formal sense, they may be right. What may be involved is a more subtle system of social agreement and pressure to buy from the domestic producer, whenever possible (as is also seen in the United States, in fact). This type of "protection" is hard to crack.

R&D support, and special investment arrangements, I suspect will continue to be employed by governments whenever these are deemed necessary to protect and sustain a home industry. I suggest that perhaps the important aims in the U.S. approach to these policies are the following. First, to gain general acceptance of the principle that as long as publicly supported research is not aimed at a particular design, the results should be open and accessible to all. Second, to press the principle that in the administration of industrial policies, domestic companies with home offices abroad should not be discriminated against. Pushing through the latter principle will be difficult in the case of Japan, but for the United States it is an objective well worth seeking.

As long as the United States is generally strong scientifically, technologically, and industrially, I suspect that we have very little to fear from the industrial policies of other countries—if we are able to get them to accept the ground rules suggested above. If the foregoing analysis is correct, as long as we stay generally strong we will not have the "frontiers" taken away from us. Being at the frontiers will enable us to meet our military national security requirements and continue to exploit our comparative advantage in manufacturing and trade. To preserve that comparative advantage requires that we do not foolishly retrench our support of academic basic scientific research, reduce funding of directed and generic research across a wide horizon of technologies in the forefront, or cut back our investment in scientific, engineering, and technological education. If we are concerned about falling behind, we ought to augment these "general industrial policies," for they can do us considerable good.

Of course, there is a danger that we may misread history, assigning too much credit to our competitors' narrow-based industrial policies and not enough to their general technological prowess. Today there are pressures to try to do what the Japanese do, whatever that may be. If I am right in my analysis, emphasizing narrow-based industrial policies never can lead to sustained technological leadership, or preserve it. Such policies are not appropriate to a country that is at the cutting edge of technological advance, as we are and as we ought to strive to continue to be.

Identifying Winners and Losers

William Nordhaus

ALTHOUGH the United States' espousal of a free market philosophy only occasionally determines its actual economic policies, a non-interventionist stance is even rarer among our trading partners. Policy interventions in recent years have often taken the grand-sounding title of "industrial policies," in part to hide their motivation or impact.

"Industrial policies" will be used here to designate measures that attempt to influence the size or growth of individual industries. As such, they exclude macroeconomic policies such as monetary or general fiscal policies. The major tools of industrial policies have been measures like tariff policies, subsidies, and such financial policies as loan guarantees.

The reasons for implementing industrial policies are varied. Often there is simply a political origin to the support of powerful lobbies, as in protecting autos or steel. There are more intellectually respectable reasons, in particular those that arise from *market failures*. A market failure arises when markets lead to incorrect or inefficient allocations. Thus, capital markets may discriminate against small firms, in which case low-interest loans might be appropriate. Natural monopolies, such as in local telephone networks, may call for control over price and entry. In my view, the most important market failure lies in the inadequacy of markets to produce sufficient new general and technical knowledge, leading to insufficient investment in R&D.

While recognizing that the real economy is rife with market failures, we must also recognize that policy responses to them may contain *political failures*. The regulation of rail, trucks, air, and natural gas in the United States was in response to perceived market failures; it is generally believed today that in these cases the regulatory apparatus was counterproductive—whatever market failures arose were less severe than the political failures. Similarly, the indirect regulation of telecommunications equipment, because the equipment manufacturer was part of a larger regulated company, undoubtedly stifled competitive pressures.

The most costly political failure is the rise of protectionist measures—tariffs, quotas, and nontariff barriers. These have little economic justification and serve mainly to redistribute income away from foreigners and domestic consumers to domestic workers and capital in protected industries.

The topic examined by this panel is a variant on issues of industrial policy. It concerns the economics and international politics of "picking winners," or singling out firms for government support and investment. The questions I will address are:

- Is picking winners just another pernicious "political failure" in the form of industrial policy?

- Are there any special lessons to be learned from the telecommunications industry?

- What, if any, guidelines should be established concerning picking winners?

Issues Relating to Picking Winners

I should state at the outset that I believe that, in general, the industrial countries' practice of picking winners is *not* enormously dangerous or costly. The practice has many forms, but there are usually two components:

- There is usually a *subsidy* arrangement whereby a domestic firm is encouraged to design and produce a new product (e.g., Concorde or System X, an electronic switch; these two examples are useful because they were actually losers).

107

- There is usually a presumption that if the subsidy produces a reasonable outcome, there will be a *procurement* preference for the product (i.e., British Air buys Concorde, British Post Office buys System X).

Thus, picking winners often involves both a subsidy and domestic protection. The mix differs as to the economic importance given to each of the two components, but both elements are often present.

My major point is that a subsidy arrangement is not particularly pernicious and may actually be useful, while a procurement preference should be avoided if possible. The reasons for beating down the attempts for domestic preference are the classical arguments in favor of a free and open trading system and will not be repeated here. But the argument for allowing or even encouraging the subsidy needs some development.

There are three reasons why a subsidy arrangement is not particularly pernicious and may be useful. The most important point is that the subsidy almost always involves encouragement of R&D or knowledge-creating activities (there are exceptions, such as agricultural subsidies). Concorde was the first commercial supersonic transport, while System X was the second electronic switch. Neither was particularly successful commercially, but both added to the knowledge of the respective technologies. Successful examples, of course, are the subsidies to computers and semiconductors in the United States which stimulated early growth; or the commercial aircraft industry, which was a spinoff from military aircraft development.

Also supporting this point is the fact that there is strong evidence that *markets underinvest in R&D*. Three NSF-sponsored studies indicate that the median social rate of return on investments in industrial R&D was about 75 percent, while the median return to the firms was 25 percent. Thus, the social rate of return to R&D appears to be many times the private rate of return.

Consequently, the major conclusion that I draw is that *the subsidy component of picking winners generally expands knowledge and is economically beneficial.*

The second reason why picking winners through subsidy is not pernicious is simply that subsidies tend to be more self-limiting than does protection. Subsidies generally involve use of public funds and receive periodic scrutiny; regulation and protection often stay in place, unchallenged, for decades.

A final reason why picking winners may be beneficial is that it is probably pro-competitive in a profound sense. To the extent that subsidies generate new technologies or new loci of activity, they increase pressure on established market power. Thus the development of communications satellites, largely by government subsidy, has led to major competitive pressures on established terrestial telecommunication carriers.

The major proviso that emerges from this discussion is that the second component of picking winners, the procurement preference for the subsidized company, generally does *not* serve a useful purpose. It is for the most part an attempt to gain export markets or inhibit imports. Indeed, in some cases (particularly the British) the raison d'être of the winner-picking is (1) to develop new products so that (2) the trade balance can be improved.

Separating the subsidy from the procurement preference may not be easy. Sometimes the subsidy is paid in the form of procurement. The German Post Office, for example, subsidized manufacturers of telecommunications equipment by including an R&D bonus in the purchase price. But the major implication of this analysis is that the protectionist aspects of picking winners should be discouraged.

Lessons from Telecommunications

One of the areas in which governments are competing actively to promote winners is telecommunications. This support ranges widely from support of basic scientific efforts (in Japan) to government subsidies of hardware (virtually everywhere outside the United States). There is virtually no explicit government support for civilian telecommunications technology in the United States.

The motivations behind the subsidies are not clear. In part there is simply a desire to promote exports. In some countries there is an apparent wish to imitate the Japanese model—i.e., policies are chosen to promote high-tech and/or high-growth industries.

Aside from the international consensus that telecommunications is an industry to be promoted, it is clear that there is a very wide variety of patterns of industrial organization and policy responses in

109

different countries. The following observations will illustrate the patterns:

1. Outside the United States there is widespread movement toward the integration of manufacturing, service, and R&D in telecommunications.* This is seen particularly in the joint ownership of R&D labs by service and manufacturing entities in Canada and Sweden. The net effect of the AT&T antitrust case in the United States is that the degree of integration in U.S. telecommunications will be less than in any major country.

2. It appears that there is widespread "user funding"† of R&D by service entities, a practice that is unique to the telephone industry. This is sometimes transparent (as in the license contract in the United States and Canada). Often there are more or less hidden government subsidies.

3. There is a very high level of R&D in the highly performing firms. Table 1 shows the most active telecommunications firms (as measured by telephony patents) and their R&D intensity. It should be noted that the R&D intensity of manufacturing in general is much lower than in the telephony firms, averaging approximately 2 percent of sales.

An even more revealing fact is that the five firms with the highest R&D intensity are *all* user-funded, while the lowest five are exclusively product-funded. This pattern suggests that a formal linkage between service entity, manufacturer, and R&D arm has been a successful way of encouraging high R&D intensities because it has encouraged user funding.

4. It is a little-known fact that most industry-financed R&D occurs in an integrated framework. Thus, about 98 percent of industry-financed R&D is actually performed by the firm that finances it. The

---

* For those not familiar with the vocabulary of telecommunications, "service" refers to the local and long-distance telephone service (such as New York Telephone Company or AT&T in the United States) ; "manufacturing" to the production of equipment (such as done by Western Electric) ; and "R&D" to the basic and applied research and development of prototypes (done by Bell Labs and by Western Electric).

† "User funding" is funding of R&D with an eye to enhancing the quality or reducing the cost of the ultimate service; this contrasts with "product funding," which signifies that the R&D is directed toward increasing the profits of the manufacturer on the product embodying the R&D.

TABLE 1 R&D Intensities of Major Telephony Firms, 1977

Rank	Company	(1) Company-funded R&D ($ millions) (1)	(2) Manufacturing sales ($ millions) (2)	R&D intensity (percent) (1)/(2) (3)
1	AT&T	$729.6	$6,914.75	10.6%
2	Bell Canada	106.3	1,001.35	10.6
3	Thomson-Brandt	444.4	4,957.72	9.0
4	L. M. Ericsson	165.3	1,997.15	8.3
5	Siemens	815.9	10,641.00	7.7
6	Philips N. V.	838.2	12,700.00	6.6
7	IBM	1,142.0	18,133.00	6.3
8	Motorola	109.0	1,847.52	5.9
9	Sony	92.3	1,830.10	5.0
10	Matsushita	251.2	6,953.60	3.6
11	Hitachi Ltd.	313.3	9,302.50	3.4
12	RCA	126.0	3,685.20	3.4
13	Zenith Radio	32.6	965.60	3.4
14	Nippon Electric	88.4	2,733.90	3.2
15	GTE	112.0	3,556.42	3.1
16	General Electric	464.0	16,805.80	2.8
17	ITT	280.0	11,885.00	2.4
18	Pioneer K. K.	14.4	738.80	1.9
19	Rockwell International	97.0	5,859.00	1.7
20	General Dynamics	34.0	2,762.44	1.2
	Average (excluding AT&T)			
	Top 20 telephony firms	290.0	6,229.00	4.7
	Next 58 telephony firms	200.0	5,176.00	3.9
	Total manufacturing	18,800.0	946,700.00	2.0

111

degree of R&D integration is even higher in technologically complex industries like communications and computers.

5. With respect to picking winners in telecommunications, there appear to be two models. One is simply to subsidize the R&D in telecomms (say, through the budget or a joint research lab, or through encouraging user funding) and allow the industry to choose the particular technology. This route appears to have been largely successful in that many innovations have arisen and have been commercial successes. The successes of Bell Labs and Bell Northern Research of Canada are well known. The results of government subsidies are less clear, but Sweden and Japan appear to have generated commercial successes from government subsidies.

6. A second model is to pick actual technologies, but this is relatively rare. In two that have been studied, the government has attempted to go outside that country's normal technique for organizing R&D. The two best known are the British System X and the German ESW system, both electronic switching systems. The first was generally thought to be inefficiently managed, but eventually produced a product. The second was a complete fiasco and was finally stopped after more than 1 billion Deutschmarks was spent.

If there is any lesson to be learned from the experience in telecommunications, it is the following: *Countries, like individuals, have very different styles of developing new ideas and incorporating them in new products. There is no dominant or uniformly successful model for organizing for rapid technical change. Perhaps the most important observation related to this is that the attempts to transplant other countries' R&D styles into an ongoing R&D organization led to waste or worse.*

Thoughts on Multilateral Efforts in High-Technology Industries

The foregoing thoughts on picking winners lead fairly naturally to some conclusions regarding the appropriate policy approaches in this area. My general view is that competition in high-technology industries is not an antisocial kind of competition. Much in the spirit of Keynes' comment, "It is better to tyrannize over one's bank account than over one's fellow man," government competition to be first in computers or telecommunications is surely to be encouraged over protectionism or, for that matter, arms sales.

With these thoughts in mind, I would suggest the following guidelines for the development of policies and discussion on a multilateral basis. First, the picking of winners should be separated into two stages—R&D subsidies and protectionist preference for domestic firms. Second, the R&D subsidy should be transparent, nontargeted, and open to all firms. Third, the protectionist element should be minimized. Once the R&D subsidy has been received, then to the maximal extent possible all domestic and foreign firms should compete on an equal basis for the final procurement contract.

And finally, the need for a new oversight mechanism to watch for abuses is fairly low on a priority list of international problems. Many other issues—classic protectionism, new nontariff barriers to trade, domestic subsidies, "pirating" of technical knowledge or products, and acid rain, to name a few—are of greater weight and deserve the scarce energy and talent of those who would set up and operate multinational institutions.

Making U.S. Trade Policy:

Government Organization, Politics,

and Interest Groups—a Survey

Harold Paul Luks

INTRODUCTION

Background

The reverberations attendant on the rise in oil prices since 1973 and the realignment of international economic relations continue to impede economic integration among the industrialized allies. A growing sense of geopolitical instability in Europe and the Middle East, combined with a widely shared perception of America's declining military and economic power, has tended to exacerbate political and economic tensions among the United States, Japan, and the European Community. The bonds of interdependence should reinforce the determination of governments to prevent problems in trade relations from developing into political disputes among allies. But countervailing domestic political pressures and the fragility of the institutions of world trade may force events into a course of continued disharmony.

One consequence of World War II was the unprecedented magnification of American economic power vis-à-vis the rest of the industrialized world. It was a unique situation because the politics of international trade was no longer closely linked to domestic political considerations. Since 1960, we have seen a dramatic growth of imports and exports as a percentage of America's Gross National Product (GNP). Today the reliance of the United States on world trade, as a portion of GNP, has yet to equal the proportion of international trade in the economies of Germany, Japan, France, Italy, or the United Kingdom even in 1960. Nevertheless, important segments of the American economy are now exposed to the caprice of exchange rate fluctuations, foreign export subsidies, regional development programs, tax incentives, and industrial policies. The current generation of American corporate officers, managers, shareholders, and politicians does not have a long enough historical memory to recall earlier days of fierce competition in world trade.

Until the late 1960s, both Congress and the executive branch largely ignored quota, tariff, and nontariff barriers in the European Economic Community and Japan which discriminated against U.S. exports or foreign investment. Nor did the political branches of government perceive potential strategic or economic problems resulting from the hemorrhage of American technology to potential political adversaries or economic competitors. For example, in the early 1950s the United States urged the Japanese to establish a "Productivity Center," similar to ones operated by Europeans, to garner advances in U.S. technology, manufacturing, and management. Democratic and Republican administrations alike encouraged the reemergence of industrial competitors. Because this objective was broadly viewed as a postwar geopolitical necessity, the United States did not use its superior economic power to seek the removal of discriminatory trade policies which did violence to the General Agreement on Tariffs and Trade (GATT). U.S. officials did not attempt to impress upon our trading partners that protectionist policies to encourage reconstruction must necessarily be only temporary expedients. Few argued at the time that a double standard in world trade would endanger the principles of the GATT charter. By the early 1970s, the Congress and the White House realized that gratitude for American postwar economic policies among nations could not be relied on as the basis for the conduct of either political or economic relations.

In examining trade relations among the industrialized allies, one principle stands above all others and imparts to the United States significant authority in any future multilateral trade negotiation: Western Europe and, particularly, Japan must have unfettered access to America's domestic marketplace. The quantitative and qualitative demands of the American market constitute, in effect, a "world market." Most trade specialists agree that the development of new technologically advanced products and services in either Japan or the European Community is predicated on the potential for American sales. It is perhaps our most important remaining trump card. In this decade, development of American import policies will be no less important than export policies to the preservation of harmonious trade relations with the industrialized countries.

Objective

The purpose of this paper is to survey the operation of political constituencies and entities which influence the course of U.S. international trade policy. The expansion of the federal government in recent years did not overlook the development and implementation of trade policy. Despite repeated attempts, even in the present administration, the trade bureaucracy seems incapable of drafting a meaningful document outlining the objectives of U.S. trade policy. A plethora of often-conflicting voices has at times produced a discordant combination of policies which have weakened America's position in trade negotiations or irritated our closest allies. This paper attempts to provide an overview of the organization of key Congressional committees, independent agencies, White House offices, and cabinet-level departments, and their emerging policies that bear on international competition, with a special reference to advanced technologies.

The paper is divided into four parts. Although the sections are interrelated, the division of topics should help to clarify how trade problems become issues in public policy. This paper does not examine the organization of federal agencies participating in the development of science and technology policy or the attitudes of Congressional committees toward that set of issues. The sections of the present paper are as follows:

A. Identification of those components of the U.S. government that contribute to the formulation of legislation governing trade in advanced technologies.

B. Survey of how those authorities define the issue and what problem areas have been identified by individual governmental authorities.

C. Evaluation of the influence of domestic constituencies (including individual high technologies such as telecommunications and microelectronics) on Congressional committees and the executive branch agencies governing trade policy.

116

D. Examination of the intragovernmental coordination process and the ability of the federal government to absorb and act upon information and recommendations from nongovernmental organizations (i.e., NAS), industry, and academia, especially in regard to trade in advanced technologies.

PART A

Organizational Structure for Trade Policy

Most administrations since 1960 have attempted to rationalize what many consider to be the ramshackle apparatus for formulating and implementing U.S. trade policy. Since the 1960s, recurring efforts at executive branch reorganization have sought to improve the interagency coordination process. Other proposals have sought to concentrate overall policy responsibility in a single board or panel within the Executive Office of the President. Every cabinet department and more than twoscore federal agencies participate in various aspects of import and export policy. Congress may yet consider proposals to either establish a separate cabinet-level trade department, strip the Department of Commerce of all components except its trade-related functions, or substantially expand the Office of the U.S. Trade Representative (USTR).

An equally unruly system prevails in the Congress. Full committees, and subcommittees with specialized jurisdiction, often compete for jurisdiction over an issue directly or indirectly connected with international trade. It is a common practice for sponsors of trade-related legislation to draft bills in such a manner that the respective parliamentarians in either the Senate or the House will direct a new bill to the author's committee. For example, recent hearings concerning international data flows, and efforts by foreign governments to restrict trade in telecommunications and information services, were held in the Subcommittee on Government Information and Individual Rights of the House Committee on Government Operations. Although the issues before the committee were international in scope, effective jurisdiction was asserted on the basis of legislation proposing executive branch reorganization.

In recent years both the Republican and Democratic leadership

117

have tended not to favor the joint referral of legislation to two or more committees. But efforts to change this practice have met with limited success. A case in point is the Foreign Corrupt Practices Act (FCPA) of 1977. This Act is widely considered, in the current administration and by a significant majority of the Congress, as an "export disincentive." However, differences among subcommittees of the House Committee on Foreign Affairs and a House Banking subcommittee regarding the Act's adverse effects on exports have impeded attempts to enact legislation. Recently, legislation to amend the FCPA by weakening its accounting controls and criminal liabilities passed the Senate by a vote of 85 to 0. It is by no means assured, however, that similar legislation to amend the Act will clear the House committees for a full debate on the floor of the House. It is one of the "protections" that characterize the unwritten system in Congress that one subcommittee chairman can either thwart or delay the enactment of legislation.

Congressional Organization

Constitutionally, the conduct of international trade and economic policy requires a high degree of interaction and cooperation between Congress and the executive branch. The President is designated by Article III of the Constitution to negotiate with foreign governments. At the same time, Article I delegates to Congress the responsibilities to "lay and collect duties" and "to regulate foreign commerce." Until the Trade Agreements Act of 1934 was signed, trade policy was essentially a matter of Congress establishing tariff schedules and the executive branch collecting the revenues. With the passage of the Trade Agreements Act (the purpose of which was to expand "foreign markets for the products of the United States"), Congress delegated broad authority to the President to negotiate and enter into trade agreements with foreign governments. Under the provisions of the Act, tariff reductions, within a specified range, and other nontariff trade agreements could be negotiated and implemented by the President without Congressional review. In the postwar period, Congress responded to an increasing perception of the importance of trade policy by gradually reasserting its authority over these matters. The Trade Act of 1974 and the Trade Agreements

Act of 1979, which constitute the foundation of current U.S. trade policy, contain specific provisions to bridge the power's delegated in Articles I and II of the Constitution. Those provisions point toward a greater degree of trust between the President and Congress regarding export policy than regarding changes in domestic laws and international agreements governing import controls.

House of Representatives

As presently constituted, four committees in the House manage most of the legislation directly concerned with international trade. Each committee is also responsible for Congressional oversight of individual executive branch and independent agencies.*

1. Committee on Ways and Means
   Oversight: U.S. Trade Representative, Treasury, Customs Service, International Trade Commission.
   Jurisdiction: All tax bills, GATT negotiations, import laws (including antidumping, countervailing duties, unfair foreign trade practices, and import relief), grants of Most Favored Nation (MFN) status, review of general and industry-specific trade policy and the various codes of the Multilateral Trade Negotiations (MTN).
   Subcommittee: International Trade.

2. Committee on Banking, Finance and Urban Affairs
   Oversight: Export-Import Bank, international lending institutions, other federal banking and securities agencies.
   Jurisdiction: International trade and investment policy, export trading companies, and hearings on trade in advanced technology products.
   Subcommittees: International Trade Investment and Monetary Policy, International Development Institutions and Finance.

3. Committee on Foreign Affairs
   Oversight: Department of Commerce (trade investment functions), Overseas Private Investment Company (OPIC), Agency for International Development (AID), Department of State, Department of Defense (military or national security-related export controls).

* Selected jurisdiction and oversight functions chosen by author.

Jurisdiction: Export promotion, export controls (including nuclear), North-South issues, foreign investment in the United States, Law of the Sea, foreign intelligence.

Subcommittees: International Economic Policy and Trade, International Security and Scientific Affairs, Europe and the Middle East.

4. Committee on Government Operations

Oversight: Jurisdiction over every agency and department within the executive branch.

Jurisdiction: Trade reorganization, Buy American laws, the MTN Code on Government Procurement.

Subcommittees: Commerce, Consumer and Monetary Affairs, Legislation and National Security.

Committee jurisdiction over the Trade Act of 1974 was predominantly concentrated within the House Committee on Ways and Means and the Senate Committee on Finance. An objective of the legislation was "to obtain more open and equitable market access and the harmonization, reduction, or elimination of devices which distort trade or commerce." To accomplish these ends Congress granted the President general authority "to negotiate structural changes in the world's trading system." This mandate enabled the United States to fully participate in the Tokyo Round of the Multilateral Trade Negotiations held between 1974 and 1979. Committee jurisdiction was clearly delineated over these GATT-related negotiations. There was a predictable absence of squabbling over who had jurisdiction regarding relief from injury caused by import competition, unfair trade practices, trade with Communist countries, and the Generalized System of Preferences (GSP).

However, competition in advanced technologies among the industrialized allies may involve committees and executive branch agencies whose primary mission is not related to international economic relations. The rules of politics do not define who would direct an examination of the interrelationships among trade, science and technology, foreign affairs, and domestic tax policy. Proposals to increase national expenditures for R&D; legislation to reconstitute a Reconstruction Finance Corporation; and proposals for the federal government to develop industrial policies may necessitate the use of joint committee hearings, multiple referrals of legislation, and expanded interagency committees. The enormous scope of these essentially domestic economic issues mitigates the ability of examining bodies to develop specific legislative proposals clearly distinguishing between ends and means.

The basic issue before the NRC panel incorporates the entire circle of problems relating to the competitiveness of the American business community in the domestic marketplace and overseas. From a political perspective, trade in advanced technology goods and services raises the question of the degree to which the federal government should expand its role in fostering the growth of certain industries through general economic policy, industry-specific policies, or special programs (which may necessitate considerable funding) to promote science, technology, and related educational programs.

House committees which could assert jurisdiction over these issues include Science and Technology, Education and Labor, Budget, Judiciary, Armed Services, and Merchant Marine and Fisheries. For example, antitrust and technological innovation, and related effects on international trade, have been the subjects of Congressional hearings. There are legislative proposals which address these issues in the Judiciary Committees. It must be kept in mind that the institutional bias of a committee could result in legislation having the opposite effect from what was envisaged by those who raised the issue in the first place. As they are presently constituted, it is difficult to imagine two committees with more opposite ideological orientations than the Judiciary Committees in the House and Senate. Their respective treatment of antitrust proposals concerning joint ventures for research would most likely result in two incompatible pieces of legislation. Thus, designing draft legislation and determining committee jurisdiction is one way to plan for favorable consideration of both issues and legislation.

Ad hoc Congressional caucuses and task forces on exports and productivity issues meet to build support for legislation or to convert specific concerns into legislative remedies. Four Congressional agencies—the Congressional Research Service, the Office of Technology Assessment, the Congressional Budget Office, and the General Accounting Office—also contribute to this ill-defined discussion process that ultimately results in the introduction of a bill and the determination of what committee and member will manage an issue.

Senate

The Senate's committee structure is similar to that of the House, but the procedures governing committee jurisdiction and the process leading toward a vote for or against a bill are quite different. The major trade committees are:

1. Finance
2. Banking, Housing and Urban Affairs
3. Foreign Relations
4. Governmental Affairs
5. Commerce, Science and Transportation

An informal review of Congressional hearings on U.S. competitiveness, parts of which include testimony on trade in advanced technologies, proved the rule that a committee or subcommittee chairman's interest—or lack thereof—in an issue is as important as actual jurisdiction. For example, in 1979, during the 96th Congress, Senator Stevenson, as chairman of the Commerce Subcommittee on Science, Technology, and Space, held a series of hearings to examine U.S. international trade over which other committees had an actual jurisdictional claim. The subcommittee hearings focused on many trade policy issues, although the legislation involved primarily domestic matters regarding R&D and innovation.

There is what amounts to a "consciousness-raising" process in Congress. Hearings can receive wide attention without focusing on specific legislation. Two joint House-Senate committees contribute to this amorphous process through which hearings, discussions, and reports shape Congressional perceptions of issues. The first is the Joint Economic Committee (JEC), which has absolutely no legislative authority but makes important contributions to the development of issues before Congress. Its hearings, reports, and nonbinding recommendations to other committees are frequently utilized by individual members to coalesce political support for legislative proposals. The second is the Joint Committee on Taxation, which does not hold hearings but publishes what many consider to be the most authoritative reports on domestic and international tax policies. Its staff testifies before all tax writing committees and its working papers are widely circulated among members and staff.

122

Executive Branch

Technically, the trade policy functions of the executive branch are explicitly enumerated in President Carter's *Reorganization Plan No. 3 of 1979*. The U.S. Trade Representative, the order reads, "shall have primary responsibility," with the advice of an interagency Trade Policy Committee, "for developing, and for coordinating the implementation of, United States international trade policy . . ." Furthermore, the USTR was designated:

as the principal advisor to the President on international trade policy and shall advise the President on the impact of other policies of the United States government on international trade . . . [to] have lead responsibility for the conduct of international trade negotiations . . . [and to] issue policy guidance to departments and agencies on basic issues of policy and interpretation . . . such guidance shall determine the policy of the United States. . . .

Other additional trade responsibilities were given to the Department of Commerce. It acquired the administration of the antidumping and countervailing duty statutes from the Treasury Department and foreign commercial representation from the Department of State. Commerce already had responsibility for export development, export controls, trade adjustment assistance, and monitoring compliance with international trade agreements. The reorganization plan thus divided policy from the actual operational responsibility for enforcing U.S. trade laws and carrying out international obligations for nonagricultural trade.

Under the provisions of the reorganization plan, the interagency Trade Policy Committee (TPC) is designated as the vehicle to "coordinate" U.S. trade policy and includes the following:

1. The U.S. Trade Representative, Chairman
2. Secretary of Commerce, Vice Chairman
3. Secretary of State
4. Secretary of the Treasury
5. Secretary of Defense
6. Attorney General
7. Secretary of the Interior
8. Secretary of Agriculture
9. Secretary of Labor

10. Secretary of Transportation
11. Secretary of Energy
12. Director of the Office of Management and Budget
13. Chairman of the Council of Economic Advisors
14. Assistant to the President for National Security Affairs
15. Director of the U.S. International Development Cooperation Agency

With few exceptions, most members of the TPC assert their claim to participate in any discussion of programs to stimulate the growth of advanced technology industries, protect the domestic market from foreign competition, or facilitate the sale abroad of advanced technology goods and services.

Two agencies, Commerce and the USTR, maintain extensive contacts with the business community through industry advisory councils. Many of their programs are informational or seek to promote exports through foreign marketing assistance. The Department of State, the Export-Import Bank, and the Small Business Administration perform similar functions which are often targeted toward a specific category of products or a specific industry, such as telecommunications, computers, information processing, and software. Departments which award federal procurement contracts are considered by some analysts to reflect in interagency deliberations the business interests of their principal contractors. In this light, within the bureaucracy a phenomenon can be observed whereby two divisions of a large corporation may advance contradictory policy positions: one seeking protection at home, and the other elimination of foreign trade barriers.

A bureaucratic overlap persists for each import or export issue. The fact that a nation's strength in high technologies is intimately related to its national security and military power has been and will continue to be a limiting factor on trade policy. While the Office of Export Administration within Commerce has the primary responsibility for regulating the sale and licensing of advanced technology, the Department of Defense is invariably an active participant in the decision to grant or deny an export license.

The sale or licensing of nuclear technologies and products is also governed by an interagency process, involving the departments of State, Commerce, Defense, and Energy, the Nuclear Regulatory

Commission, and the Arms Control and Disarmament Agency. Products of advanced research, including pesticides and pharmaceuticals, that are classified as hazardous substances are subject as well to export controls administered by both the Environmental Protection Agency and the Food and Drug Administration.

Regulation of import competition and relief from unfair foreign trade practices are divided among five agencies: USTR, Commerce, Labor, the International Trade Commission (ITC), and the Customs Service. U.S. domestic laws to protect American business, workers, and consumers from unfair foreign trade practices are bounded by four sections of U.S. trade law. These are:

1. Antidumping Act of 1921 and 1916, as amended
2. Countervailing Duty Law of 1897, as amended
3. Section 337 of the Tariff Act of 1930, as amended
4. Section 301 of the Trade Act of 1974

The Antidumping Act and Countervailing Duty Law both have long histories of adjudication and administrative decision-making. Much has been written about the effectiveness of these laws in protecting domestic industries. However, the number of cases decided and thus the precedents established under Sections 337 and 301 have been significantly fewer. The potential of these laws to control importation of goods could be expanded with Presidential or Congressional initiatives.

Section 337 is administered by the ITC, Commerce, and the President, and can result in import restrictions. The ITC investigates

alleged unfair methods of competition or unfair acts in the importation of articles [or the sale of stocks in the United States]. The Commission investigates to determine whether such methods or acts are being practiced, and whether such methods or acts have the effect or tendency of destroying or substantially injuring an efficiently and economically operated U.S. industry, preventing the establishment of a U.S. industry, or restraining or monopolizing trade or commerce in the United States.

Section 301 is designed to enforce U.S. trading rights in trade agreements. It imparts to the President broad authority to retaliate against "unreasonable" and "unjustifiable" foreign import restrictions and export subsidies.

[Unjustifiable is defined as] restrictions which are illegal under international law or inconsistent with international obligations. Unreasonable

125

refers to restrictions which are not necessarily illegal but which nullify or impair benefits accruing to the United States under trade agreements or which otherwise discriminate against or burden U.S. commerce.

This broad language of both statutes is delimited by the findings of the ITC. The importance of this small, independent agency and its unique relationship to Congress will be discussed in Part D of this paper. Suffice it at this point to note that some political representatives, and certain members of the business community, would favor a new and more restrictive mechanism than currently in force based on Sections 301 and 337 to limit the access of foreign competitors to the U.S. market. This would be a more effective mechanism, they contend, than multilateral or bilateral trade negotiations to regulate international commerce and would effectively protect U.S. industry from "unfair" foreign trade practices.

In the area of foreign investment, restrictions on the activities of U.S. firms and multinationals may be as important as the competitiveness of an industry or its efforts to develop export sales. The Treasury Department continues, with the advice of State and USTR, to have major policy and negotiating responsibilities. Current practice designates Treasury to lead the U.S. representation at the Committee on Capital Movements and Invisible Transactions of the Organization for Economic Cooperation and Development (OECD) and to chair the interagency Committee on Foreign Investment in the United States.

President Reagan has chosen to continue the President's Export Council (PEC), composed of seven departments and agencies, three members from both Houses of Congress, and not more than twenty-eight representatives from business, industry, agriculture, and labor. The PEC is authorized to examine export problems and to make specific recommendations to the President. The PEC has become the focus of considerable attention in the business community. There are questions as to whether it possesses the institutional resources and political clout to influence policy, and whether other trade agencies seek to limit its access to the President.

Clearly, USTR and Department of Commerce should be the focus for the making of trade policy. In practice, the substantive policy organization of the executive branch is opaque. The newly established White House Cabinet Council on Trade and Commerce and the Senior Interagency Groups added additional layers to the decision-making bureaucracy. With fewer than 113 employees, USTR cannot assert its mandate for leadership throughout the bowels of the trade bureaucracy. U.S. efforts in 1981 to obtain a voluntary restraint agreement from Japan for limiting auto exports provided one example of USTR's institutional weakness vis-à-vis other agencies. During auto import talks with the Japanese, Presidents Carter and Reagan's intervention was necessary to defend USTR's negotiating role from encroachment by the Secretaries of State, Commerce, and Transportation.

Finally, since the early 1970s intermittent reports and Congressional hearings have raised the question of advanced technology competition among the industrialized allies. The issue has largely been viewed in the context of domestic economic policy. Additionally, in the post-MTN era, both the Carter and Reagan administrations have raised the issue of international trade in services as the next subject for multilateral consideration. Yet no one agency, department, or Congressional committee has specifically drawn together the convergent issues which relate to international competition in advanced technologies. What may be necessary is for one leading Administration official actually to begin talking about the issue.

PART B

In December 1971, Peter G. Peterson, Assistant to the President and Executive Director of the Council on International Economic Policy (CIEP), submitted two reports: *A Foreign Economic Perspective* and *The United States in the Changing World Economy*. Earlier that year a three-volume report, *United States International Economic Policy in an Interdependent World*, was forwarded to President Nixon by the Commission on International Trade and Investment Policy.

That same year, articles appeared in leading journals about the possibilities of a trade war with the European Economic Community (EEC). The CIEP report pointed to several indications that the U.S. economy, in certain key industrial sections, was losing its competitive edge. In 1971, the Commission on International Trade and Investment Policy focused on a number of issues outstanding between the United States and the EEC, most of which still perplex the political establishment and the American business community. These issues included exceptions to the principle of nondiscrimina-

127

tion and MFN, restrictions on imports from Japan, preferential trade agreements, government procurement, nontariff barriers (e.g., standards and other technical barriers to trade), and the effects of industrial policies on international trade. Three problems regarding Japan were considered by the commission: the nature of her competitive edge, the response of the industrialized nations, and the "speed and effectiveness of Japan's programs of import liberalization." The commission's recommendations are applicable today: the United States should (a) urge Japan to eliminate restrictive import practices, including "administrative guidance" and (b) press for "full freedom of entry for foreign direct investment."

The broad policy issues and technical problems in trade administration now before Congress and the executive branch were defined in the 1960s and 1970s. Some of the problems found expression in the codes of the Multilateral Trade Negotiation to reduce the distorting effects of nontariff barriers. Strengthening the international dispute settlement provisions of each code, however, will require specific undertakings by the executive branch to pursue trade cases in Geneva. Congress, through oversight hearings, can ascertain the effects of each code (e.g., Governmental Procurement, Customs Valuation, Licensing, Standards, Aircraft), but cannot alter the terms of the agreement without risking the demise of the trade structure of the MTN. As competition in advanced technologies intensifies, there will be increasing pressure to resolve disputes without regard for the GATT or the MTN. The pattern is already well established in steel, textiles, televisions, and other products. Governments increasingly tend to negotiate voluntary restraint agreements (VRAs) and orderly marketing agreements (OMAs). Short-term trade disputes are settled without addressing long-term issues of competitiveness, and the parties bypass the formal requirements of the GATT which work to limit restraints on international trade.

Both political branches of government recognize that serious strains over trade policy are developing, not only with Japan, but also with the European Community. Our trade surplus with the European Community may surpass $20 billion for 1981. Possible U.S. government action to limit imports of European Community steel, American pressure to restrain sales to Communist countries in Eastern Europe, the breakdown of the "gentlemen's agreement" among industrialized countries to reduce subsidized export credits, differences over U.S. interest rates and their effect on exchange rates, and recurring complaints from Washington regarding the EEC's Common Agricultural Policy continue to inject discord in transatlantic economic relations.

Statements in the *Congressional Record* and recent hearings indicate that many influential members of Congress perceive a set of interrelated trade crises. The first is the flagging performance of the U.S. economy. The second is the inability to correct in the short term the fundamental problems associated with declining international competitiveness. Third, long-term policies to strengthen certain sectors of the economy will require expenditures that are excessive in light of current budgetary restrictions and the financial costs to the Treasury of recent changes in tax policy. Fourth, political pressure to shield so-called declining and growth industries from the impact of foreign competition may impel a new coalition in Congress and among selected executive branch agencies, to press for "protectionist" policies. The continued departure from unconditional MFN, and the weapon of selected retaliation to limit the importation of items from only one country, is a policy under active Congressional discussion. (Major precedents in this general direction were the MTN codes in which the benefits of the codes devolve only to signatories.)

The plethora of books and articles about causes of Japan's economic success continue to emphasize industry-specific targeting for export growth. Japan's Ministry of International Trade and Investment's report "The Vision of MITI Policies in the 1980s" was widely circulated on Capitol Hill and within the executive branch. That "Japan must stand on the ground of technology" and the accompanying outline of specific goals for science and technology policy in this decade have contributed to political fear, frustration, and envy of the Japanese. In the past, the executive branch has served as a brake on protectionist sentiment in Congress—but this pattern may now be breaking down.

Curiously, much less attention has been given to the U.S. trade balance with West Germany and the efforts of German firms to restore competitiveness in certain technologies. Unlike the MITI report, the EEC's May 1981 Declaration calling for policies to promote the development in Europe of advanced technologies went largely unnoticed in Congress, although its successful implementation would work against U.S. commercial interests.

129

Most people in government and the business community would agree that innovation, R&D, and productivity are the three pillars of competitiveness. In the 1950s and 1960s, national defense was the vehicle by which a great many changes in government planning, policies, and organization were effected. In the late 1970s and the 1980s, trade and competitiveness were increasingly used as justifications for major changes in domestic economic policy. These concepts provide a convenient means of explaining domestic economic weaknesses, although the origin of these weaknesses is not strictly international.

Trade regulation introduced in the 96th and 97th Congresses concentrated in nine issue areas: export credit financing, antitrust policy, export disincentives, trade with nonmarket economies, export promotion, tax policy, trade reorganization, amendments to laws governing imports, and amendments to laws governing agriculture. Other proposals, which could be classified as "productivity enhancement legislation" (including domestic tax law proposals), easily exceeded two hundred bills. Perhaps the most significant factor was the absence of any Presidential activity in the area of proposing (formally or informally) legislation on a major aspect of trade policy. Political initiatives (e.g., to shape science and technology policy) that cut across the jurisdiction of Congressional committees and executive branch agencies appear doomed to bureaucratic obfuscation unless Presidential and Congressional leaders agree in advance on specific procedures and timetables. Such agreement was a major reason for the expeditious consideration of the MTN legislation in Congress.

PART C

In the jargon of trade politics, "reciprocal trade" and "fair trade" have effectively replaced "free trade" as an objective of United States policy. With the political changes brought about in Congress by the 1980 elections, there are few Senators or Congressmen who openly defend the basic premises of a liberal trade policy. Few politicians now publicly state that free trade is the best policy to expand the nation's wealth, maintain domestic competition, create jobs, or curtail inflationary pressures. Instead, the argument is couched in terms of supporting an open international trading system while at the same time being prepared to retaliate against unfair foreign trade practices. This "practical" approach to trade policy rejects the notion that the rigors of the international marketplace should determine the survival or destruction of domestic industries. As a practical matter, the attention of the political establishment, through the activities of organized labor and business, is more clearly focused on "declining" than on growing or emerging industries. In fact, even the most liberal free traders in Congress are not prepared to witness the demise of basic industries in autos, steel, and apparel.

It is also no accident that the chairman of the Ways and Means Trade Subcommittee from Florida was outspoken regarding Japanese restrictions on citrus exports or that his counterpart in the Senate, with major auto assembly plants in his state, was active regarding imports of foreign cars.

However, political considerations and trade politics are not necessarily pejorative terms. Representatives of districts experiencing growth via high-technology industries have been influenced by business constituencies to support an activist export policy and to work for the removal of foreign trade barriers. Yet these same industry coalitions are apprehensive about the potential adverse effects of foreign competition and industrial targeting, whether or not there are allegations of unfair trade practices.

Responding to industry concerns and pressures in 1978, two Senate trade committees requested the ITC to undertake a study of international trade in integrated circuits. The commission's report was one of the most comprehensive examinations of world trade in one product ever undertaken by a U.S. government authority. It concluded that the U.S. "chip" industry would (1) continue to expand, (2) maintain its position as the world's leading producer and innovator, and (3) maintain profitability. Following publication of the commission's findings, industry warnings of foreign competition temporarily subsided. Within a year, however, new dangers were pointed out to Congress by industry spokesmen regarding Japanese production of telecommunications and information-processing equipment.

Interest groups wishing to restrict imports (e.g., organized labor and labor-management coalitions for import-sensitive industries) have identifiable problems from their perspective and can thus present to Congress and the President specific proposals for import relief. They can also point to defects in the administration and enforcement of U.S. trade laws that, in their view, have significantly

131

contributed to severe reductions in the size of domestic industries. Finally, those domestic constituencies which favor "protection" tend to become vocal supporters of Congressional coalitions with a willingness to be receptive to the industry's point of view.

Those constituencies that support a liberal trade order rely first and foremost on the tradition of Congressional and executive branch communication and cooperation to limit protectionist tendencies. Major manufacturers of aircraft, computers, telecommunications systems, electrical generating equipment, machine tools, and heavy capital goods have the strength of export figures and their positive contribution to the balance of payments to support their cause. These companies and U.S.-based multinationals are highly organized and can afford the best legal talent and former government officials to work toward their goals, which are:

1. the removal of foreign trade barriers;
2. the elimination of U.S. export disincentives;
3. the preservation of U.S. government programs which benefit foreign operators and sales;
4. minimum restrictions on the sale or licensing of advanced technologies; and
5. the elimination of overseas barriers to U.S. foreign investment.

These industries and their lobbies, such as the Business Roundtable and the smaller Emergency Committee for American Trade, rarely dilute their energies by opposing the trade concessions and restraints which other industries request from Congress or the President. They are, however, compelled to defend the operation of the Domestic International Sales Corporation, the foreign tax credit, and funding for the Export-Import Bank. Congressional critics, consumer groups, and organized labor consistently attack these programs as either unnecessary export subsidies or violations of the GATT.

When faced with the possibility that adverse policies will be instituted by either the President or Congress, the major corporations can in short order orchestrate a major campaign to defend their interests. When President Reagan proposed a reduction in the Export-Import Bank funding, he faced solid opposition in Congress. The fact that a labor-management coalition of these high-technology industries and major exporters presented their case on Capitol Hill contributed to Congress's revising the President's budget request.

Since the passage of the Trade Act of 1974, a new factor has altered the pattern of interest-group lobbying. The Act provided for the creation of industrial-sector advisory groups. Never before in U.S. trade history have so many committees and so many individuals been given the mandate to participate in shaping the negotiating posture of the United States. Forty-five advisory committees and nearly one thousand participants from companies large and small and from labor, agriculture, local governments, and consumer groups were requested, in effect, to lobby their government regarding trade policy. This institutionalized safety valve resulted in certain accommodations with proponents of protectionist policies. At the same time, it also ensured the overwhelming passage of the MTN agreements into U.S. law. Such government-labor-industry committees, constituted on an industry-specific basis, have the potential of developing policies on issues even beyond the actual conduct of trade negotiations.

PART D

With rare exceptions, the Congressional and executive branch paper flow on international trade bypasses Senators, Congressmen, cabinet secretaries, and undersecretaries. It passes unbeknownst to most Congressional staff; only a portion is reviewed by individuals on personal and committee staffs. It is probable that not more than twenty-five Congressional staff were intimately involved in drafting the legislation to implement the Tokyo Round. The bureaucracies cajole and argue among themselves, through interagency committees, to shape the day-to-day operation of export and import policy. In most cases, Congress becomes involved after the executive branch, through the President, has already made its intentions known.

Although there are exceptions to the rule, traditionally the departments of State and Treasury, the Council of Economic Advisers, the Office of Management and Budget, and USTR denigrate protectionism and rely instead on market forces to determine international competitiveness. The departments of Commerce and Labor tend to follow a course more sympathetic to import restraints and to the concepts of fair trade and reciprocity. Such divisions are somewhat artificial because the President, as the ultimate arbiter of trade policy, can overrule bureaucratic recommendations or policy initiatives.

The making of trade policy is conditioned by a fear of what a return to protectionism would entail for the U.S. economy. Therefore, despite policy differences and despite their sensitivity to the diplomatic consequences of trade policy, more often than not the President and Congress feel constrained to trust each other's good intentions. Congressional sensitivity to the institutional bias of an agency is quite realistic. It removed antidumping and countervailing responsibilities from Treasury because it believed that domestic industries would receive a more favorable review of their petitions by the Department of Commerce. The same awareness explains why the Senate wants the business-oriented Department of Commerce to make certain determinations under the Foreign Corrupt Practices Act (FCPA), rather than the Department of Justice and the Security and Exchange Commission.

Congress is generally considered to be more inclined toward protectionism than is the President. Even so, Congress has been reluctant to determine on its own when the President should be compelled to impose import restraints or retaliate against unfair foreign trade practices.

Perhaps Congressional awareness of its collective bias toward protectionism is reflected in the charter of the ITC. The charter was drafted by Congress to prevent the commission from becoming a partisan political body or one dominated by the President. Its six commissioners are appointed by the President and confirmed by the Senate for a single term of nine years. To further guarantee its independence from the President, the ITC's budget is established directly by Congress, a procedure unique in the federal government. The 1974 and 1979 trade bills vested the ITC with new responsibility to expand its investigatory powers. Its examination of trade issues takes place in the framework of a public and quasijudicial process. Yet the decisions and recommendations of the ITC regarding import restrictions are often overridden by the President.

Patience and persistence are cardinal virtues in making trade policy. The cumulative effect of constant repetition of ideas is eventually felt. Private conferences, the reports of nongovernmental organizations, agency reports and memorandums, academic journals and books, occasional texts like the *American Challenge* or *Japan as Number One*, and publications of the Office of Technology Assessment, the Commission on International Relations of the National

Academy of Sciences, and the National Science Foundation are transmitted in ever more digested form to those in high leadership positions. For instance, Congressional speed in enacting the 1981 Economic Recovery Act was greatly facilitated by overlapping events in Congress and in the executive branch, prior to 1980 promoting supply-side economics. The fact that the 1980 report of the House-Senate Joint Economic Committee (JEC), signed by every Democratic and Republican member of the committee, was entitled "Plugging in the Supply Side" illustrates how the constant repetition of new themes from so many sources had influenced both chambers. In a similar vein, numerous reports and conferences elevated Congressional and Presidential concern that the United States was not holding its own in world markets. Whether this assessment is well founded or not, leading members of Congress, or cabinet officers, might now be receptive to a new trade policy. In the absence of Presidential initiatives, an authoritative nongovernmental body could add substance and direction to governmental consideration of trade policy.

APPENDIX

Conclusions Regarding Trade Studies

The studies selected for this section, and the record of one series of hearings, reflect the quality and diversity of research on trade-related issues. Several conclusions can be drawn from these kinds of studies:

- In several instances, the conclusions and implied policy recommendations of the studies were at variance with legislative trends.

- Because of the number of participants, interagency reports tend to seek the lowest common denominator for determining policy recommendations.

- Rarely does the executive branch engage in the candor often found in the reports of the General Accounting Office or the Office of Technology Assessment.

- The goal of searching for consensual positions dilutes the effect of joint institutional studies.

135

• Major studies with important policy implications will not find their way into the legislative process unless communicated to the leadership and staff of the Congress and the executive branch.

Selected Studies

1. *Manufacturing Technology—A Changing Challenge to Improved Productivity*. General Accounting Office, Washington, D.C., 1976. Report Number ICD-75-436.
    This study was the first government review of computer-integrated manufacturing and its effects on domestic industrial productivity and international trade. It highlighted the rapidly increasing use of such manufacturing processes abroad, particularly in Japan. GAO surveyed two hundred U.S. companies and found that "the use of these advanced methods is almost nonexistent" among them. GAO investigators reported on funding by foreign governments for advanced technologies to sustain their international competitiveness in a variety of capital goods, including machine tools (where, incidentally, the United States has been losing its share of world markets). It examined inter alia changing economic conditions; Japan's business environment; productivity and its relationship to antitrust; educational policies; the problems associated with capital spending; and the quantity and character of national expenditures for R&D. The authors cite a 1973 GAO report entitled "Clarifying Webb-Panerene Act Needed to Help Increase U.S. Exports." Now, more than *eight years* after its publication, Congress is still debating the merits of expanding opportunities for export trading companies. Similarly, public officials still speak of foreign leadership in "robotics" when the warning signal was sounded several years ago.

2. *United States–Japan Trade: Issues and Problems*. General Accounting Office, Washington, D.C., 1979. Report Number ID-79-53.
    Following its release, this report received wide Congressional attention and was the subject of a JEC hearing. The study examined those indicators which are often cited to support the

thesis of declining U.S. competitiveness; its authors stated that "Japan encourages its strong industries; the United States protects its weak ones." This study compares and contrasts Japanese and American domestic tax, regulatory and investment policies. The body of the report consists of seven case studies of Japanese industries (e.g., computers, telecommunications, and machine tools). Apropos of current trade negotiations with Japan, the study concludes that Tokyo has dismantled most tariff and nontariff business.

The report seems to suggest that current efforts to eliminate remaining non-tariff barriers may be a diversion from the overriding issue of how to manage competition in advanced technology products.

3. *Competitive Factors Influencing World Trade in Integrated Circuits.* U.S. International Trade Commission, Washington, D.C., 1979. USITC Publication 1013 on Investigation No. 332-102.
The ITC's study is a public version of a confidential study. It is the most comprehensive economic and technical analysis of a high-technology industry confronted with increasing foreign competition prepared by an agency of the U.S. government. The commission made the following points which should influence any attempt to develop a national development strategy for this industry: (a) the loss of world market shares was due to limited production facilities, caused by under-investment; (b) technology transfer also contributes to this loss; (c) foreign investment in the United States will likely increase, and this will be predominantly from Western Europe; (d) U.S. companies will face increased competition in Japan, in their own market, and in Western Europe; and (e) foreign governments are investing considerable sums to develop technologies and products that are directly competitive with U.S. products.

4. *Report of the President on U.S. Competitiveness; Together with the Study on U.S. Competitiveness.* U.S. Department of Labor, Office of Foreign Economic Research. U.S. Government Printing Office, Washington, D.C., 1980. Includes "Trends in Technology-Intensive Trade," published separately as Eco-

nomic Discussion Paper 9, the Bureau of International Trade Affairs.

This study was mandated by Congress in the 1979 Trade Agreements Act. The conclusions were hardly startling. U.S. export strength relies on high-value-added advanced technology products. It confirmed existing data that the United States suffers from a serious lag in capital spending. Discussion of productivity issues concentrates on the importance of R&D and industrial innovation. Yet there seems to be an internal weakness in the failure to ascertain the results of foreign government spending for R&D—particularly with reference to the United Kingdom, which has devoted a very high percentage of GNP to R&D but has a poor record of converting R&D activities into expanded market shares. Nevertheless, the report is one of the few sources to collect and organize a vast array of data on trade, productivity, R&D, and industrial innovation issues.

The section titled "Technology Intensive Trade" is a useful review of the sources of U.S. comparative advantage and the endogenous and exogenous factors which will contribute to increased competition and a loss of market shares in the industrialized and developing countries.

5. *Export Promotion, Export Disincentives, and U.S. Competitiveness.* Committee on Banking, Housing and Urban Affairs. U.S. Senate, 95th Congress, Second Session. Committee Print, September 1980. U.S. Government Printing Office, Washington, D.C., 1980.

The Department of Commerce and USTR supervised the preparation of this interagency report. Although it was required by the Trade Agreements Acts, interagency disagreements prevented the study from becoming a statement of administration policy. The substance of the study is a catalogue of complaints about disincentives (e.g., taxation of Americans overseas, antitrust issues, the FCPA) ; yet on a different level the study is an example of how government and business resources can come to be devoted to a series of issues which, in and of themselves, do not (according to the empirical evidence) seriously hinder the ability of American business to compete overseas. In fact, the authors of the study did not attempt to quantify the costs of the disincentives under review.

A parallel study is the 1980 *Report of the President's Export Council.* Both documents are basic summaries of government and business views regarding U.S. trade policy.

6. *Technology and Steel Industry Competitiveness.* Congress of the United States. Office of Technology Assessment. U.S. Government Printing Office, Washington, D.C., 1980.

   This report is a case study of what U.S. business, in cooperation with the federal government, could accomplish to restore the competitiveness of the U.S. steel industry. The course suggested is increased investment in R&D and the adoption of new technologies. Companies would have to substantially increase capital spending, with part of the cost for R&D (including pilot and demonstration projects) being borne by the federal government. OTA presented to Congress a long-term strategic plan for technological development to preserve the viability of a basic industry—and one vital to national security. The report has received modest attention in Congress. A more perplexing problem is why the administration has not used the OTA report to garner the political capital such a revitalization program would engender.

7. Hearings held on Industrial Innovation by the Senate committees on Commerce, Science and Transportation and on Small Business, and House committees on Science and Technology and on Small Business. October 31 and November 14, 1979. Committee Print, 96th Congress, First Session. U.S. Government Printing Office, Washington, D.C., 1979.

   These hearings illustrate how a small number of Members of Congress can compel the examination of an issue. The hearings reviewed R&D and industrial innovation, productivity growth, technology and international competitiveness, and specific government policies regarding tax, regulatory, and antitrust policies. The testimony of witnesses and the questions of the members helped to delineate policy issues.

   These hearings demonstrated that despite the defects of the hearing process, careful preparation by committee staffs working with private sector and nongovernmental organizations can establish a forum for "educating" members of Congress, business, and the public to the importance of these long-term policy issues.

U.S. Trade Policy and Industrial
Policies: Related Problems Regarding
U.S. Competitiveness

Harold Paul Luks

INTRODUCTION

"Japan must stand on the ground of technology" and "technological developments must be promoted by presenting a long-term vision . . . which identifies the priority goals for technological developments, as well as systems for development and funding. . . . the government must launch national projects on its own initiatives." These quotations from *The Vision of MITI Policies in the 1980s,* released in March 1980 by Japan's Ministry of International Trade and Industry, outline a combination of industrial policies to achieve economic security through technological innovation.

Particularly for the Japanese, public policy does not recognize categorical distinctions between domestic economic and international trade policy. In Japan since the late 1960s, and more recently in the European Community, there is a recognition by government and many industries that cooperative relationships are a necessity to establish national goals to meet the economic adjustments resulting from a "third technological revolution," also known as the "postindustrial society." Retrospectively, it appears that the Japanese government deliberately guided industrial development by establishing objectives, removing obstacles, and providing incentives for its industries. Whether such "industrial policies" are significantly responsible for Japan's success in certain export industries is a debatable issue.* Unlike the United States, Western European and Japanese govern-

---

* Terutoma Ozawa, *Japan's Technological Challenge to the West, 1950–54* (Cambridge: MIT Press, 1974); Ira C. Magaziner and Thomas M. Hout, *Japanese Industrial Policy* (London: Policy Studies Institute, 1980).

ments, although constrained in many instances by domestic political circumstances, seek to consciously target the development of certain industries at the expense of other industries.

The intimacy which industrial policies imply between domestic economic performance and international competitiveness only recently in the United States has gained a recognition in the circles of government. Interest in industrial policy has increased with the failures attributed to the ability of macroeconomic policy to control inflation, to create adjustment policies as basic industries decline, to sustain the international competitiveness of American manufacturers, and to avoid the economic and social disruptions caused by unemployment.

Except in the most general terms, no agency of the federal government has produced "A Vision of U.S. Economic and Trade Policies for the 1980s." However, legislative and executive branch proposals for economic recovery, revitalization, reindustrialization, a national science and technology policy, or a national export policy are at least euphemisms for industrial policies. U.S. trade policy provides the impetus to this development.

Beginning in 1934, Congress approved a series of Reciprocal Trade Agreements which authorized the President to negotiate successive and mutually beneficial *tariff reductions* with America's trading partners. Since that time, five additional elements of U.S. trade policy, some of which may appear contradictory as a mixture of free trade and protectionism, have emerged to encompass:

- participation in multilateral institutions to strengthen and expand a liberal world trading system;

- utilization of both multilateral and bilateral negotiations to develop standards of international trade practice to reduce nontariff barriers to trade;

- development and enforcement of legal mechanisms to protect American industry and workers from unfair or injurious foreign competition (e.g., antidumping, countervailing duties, escape clause);

- initiation of bilateral agreements, and participation in multilateral agreements, to restrict exports to the United States and/or to allocate market shares (e.g., Orderly Marketing Agreements, Voluntary Restraint Agreements); and

141

- organizing export promotion and expansion programs (including the activities of the Department of Commerce, EXIM, and OPIC).

Objectives and Methodology

There are two parts to this paper. The objective of the first part is to catalogue and examine the legislative proposals regarding trade policy which have the effect of potentially restricting foreign sales in the U.S. market and other proposals designed to stimulate exports or to negotiate the reduction of foreign trade barriers to U.S. exports and foreign investment. Much of this legislation amends existing statutes which confer, on either the President, Congress, or independent agencies, the ability to control various aspects of U.S. import or export policy.

The second part surveys certain federal programs and policies, and a number of legislative proposals, within the context of a de facto U.S. industrial policy. Increasingly, proposals to change loan credit and guarantee programs, procurement policies, patent and trademark law, and the Internal Revenue Code make reference to America's competitive posture in world markets. Part B of this paper looks at a number of domestic economic programs which allocate federal resources to one industry or region at the expense of another. The listing of programs is not comprehensive but illustrative of how ostensibly nontrade endeavors of the U.S. government affect U.S. competitiveness.

PART A: LEGISLATION FOR CONTROL OF IMPORT AND EXPORT POLICY

Protectionism During the Carter Administration

As an institution, Congress rarely distinguishes during its deliberations on trade policy between the current account balance and the overall balance of payments. Trade deficits, and a declining U.S. share of world exports in manufactured goods and services, are seen by many in Congress as positive indicators that U.S. exports confront unfair and "illegal" foreign discrimination or that the U.S. economy is losing its competitive edge.* The political repercussions of persistent trade deficits since 1975 reinforced this view and resulted in a bipartisan consensus in Congress to reduce the tax and regulatory burden on U.S. industry so as to stimulate productivity, R&D, and technological innovation, and thereby restore America's ability to compete abroad.†

The conclusion of the Tokyo Round of Multilateral Trade Negotiations (MTN) to liberalize world trade and the enactment of the Trade Agreements Act of 1980 tends to overshadow other less progressive trade legislation during the Carter presidency. Throughout 1977 and 1978 the administration increasingly emphasized the need to conclude the MTN negotiations. In his 1980 State of the Union address the President said: "We expect to achieve major reductions in tariff and nontariff barriers to international trade. . . . It will be critical to the health of our domestic economy and of the world economy."

Yet on two occasions Congress nearly scuttled the MTN. In the final days of the 95th Congress in October 1978, Senator Hollings (D.-S.C.) offered an amendment to prohibit the reduction or elimination of U.S. tariffs on textiles and textile products during the MTN. The result, he predicted, would be "to risk losing all the work and all the possible benefits of an improved international trading system just because one sector wants to be treated differently from any other sector of the economy." The Hollings proposal overwhelmingly passed both the Senate and House. It was vetoed by President Carter.

The second instance involved extension of the President's authority to waive the collection of countervailing duties (CVD) primarily involving imports from Western Europe. Upon entering the Tokyo Round, Congress suspended the collection of countervailing duties intended to offset foreign export subsidies which injured U.S. companies and workers. A further extension was necessary until the conclusion of the MTN negotiations. Danish canned hams and butter cookies accounted for approximately one-half of the $600 million in affected imports, an amount which was less than 1 percent of total

---

* U.S. Senate, Committee on Finance, *Conference on U.S. Competitiveness: Can the United States Remain Competitive?*, 96th Congress Committee Print 96-38. (Washington: GPO, 1980).
† N.Y. Stock Exchange, *U.S. Economic Performance in a Global Perspective* (New York: NYSE, 1981), supports this thesis.

U.S. trade with Western Europe. Organized labor, certain agricultural interests, and the textile lobby testified against the waiver extension, making it clear that a vote for or against the waiver was also a vote for or against the MTN. It was also clear that the Europeans would cancel the MTN if Congress failed to extend the President's waiver authority. One bill to extend the CVD waiver failed in the 95th Congress. Not until the administration granted concessions to the dairy and textile industries did Congress act affirmatively.

These events illustrate that combinations of industries with powerful allies in Congress could reorient trade policy from liberalization to protectionism. Other examples of protectionist legislation during the 96th Congress addressed steel and specialty steel imports and the importation of automobiles from Japan. Majorities in both houses were on record before the inauguration of Ronald Reagan calling on the President to negotiate an export restraint agreement with the Japanese. Several other proposals specifically limited the quantity of Japanese cars imported into the United States during 1981–1985. Although temporarily rendered moot by Japan's "voluntary" agreement to restrict auto exports, these same bills could be resubmitted with semiconductors, telecommunications equipment, or construction machinery substituted for automobiles.

The auto import legislation was protectionist for several reasons. First, the bills selectively sought to restrict the product of one country, a measure not in accord with the articles of GATT, which do not favor selective retaliation. Second, import restrictions would be imposed outside the established framework of U.S. import relief laws which permit the President to restrict imports if agencies of the U.S. government determine that imports are being subsidized, are being dumped, or are injuring U.S. workers or firms, or that U.S. exports are being unreasonably or unjustifiably restricted from a foreign market. Third, Congressionally mandated selective retaliation ignores international trade dispute settlement procedures. Fourth, unilateral action by the United States would have severe repercussions on multilateral negotiations to reach agreement on a Safeguards Code, which was the major unresolved issue of the Tokyo Round.

Throughout the MTN negotiations, the Europeans insisted that the proposed Safeguards Code permit importing nations to selectively restrict imports of particular products from one or two countries instead of limiting imports on a most-favored-nation basis from all suppliers. American negotiators joined with the developing countries and Japan to oppose selective retaliation. According to a senior trade specialist in Congress, the distance was not great between selective retaliation and the unilateral action by Congress to restrict imports.

An emerging consensus in the 96th Congress that U.S. exports faced "unfair competition" led to enactment of several measures to ostensibly strengthen America's competitive position overseas. Congress appropriated additional export credits (from $25 billion to $40 billion) for the Export-Import Bank (EXIM) and the Commodity Credit Corporation to challenge foreign "subsidized" export credits. Many trade observers contended that foreign "below-market" export credits were displacing U.S. capital goods exports in Third World markets. Congress rejected President Carter's call for repeal of the Domestic International Sales Corporation (DISC) and the President's argument that the DISC was an inefficient expenditure of tax dollars to boost exports. However, the President requested tax relief (Sections 911 and 913 of the IRS Code) for Americans living and working overseas. In this instance, Congress exceeded the President's request and granted nearly $250 million in tax reductions on the premise that export performance was related to the numbers of American citizens working abroad for U.S. companies. Amending 911 and 913 was one of several examples where Congress acted to bring U.S. laws into greater conformity with incentives provided by foreign governments to their nationals.

Increasing reference was also made in Congress to trade policies of U.S. competitors which, if adopted by Congress, would depart from traditional U.S. practice. The various Export Trading Company (ETC) bills are one example. First, the ETC proposals overturn nearly five decades of legal separation between commerce and commercial banking. Second, ETCs would benefit from liberalized enforcement of the antitrust laws, in effect permitting certain kinds of conduct overseas which would remain domestically illegal. Third, Senate proponents of ETCs would permit the inclusion of all services within the scope of ETCs and extend to them the tax benefits of the DISC.*

---

* At the time of writing of this paper it appears likely that for reasons of cost, enforcement, and the expected adverse reaction of the Europeans, who oppose the DISC, this section of the bill will not pass.

Another trend in the 96th Congress was seen in attempts to limit the effects of or to repeal so-called export disincentives. These included liberalization of trade with nonmarket Communist countries and, until the invasion of Afghanistan, modification of the Jackson-Vanik Amendment, which makes U.S. extension of Most Favored Nation (MFN) status to the Soviet Union contingent upon Presidential certification of free emigration from the USSR. Until Afghanistan, many trade advocates in Congress pressed for liberalization of export control regulations restricting the transfer to communist countries of militarily significant goods and technology. Except for the outspoken opposition of its author, not a single Senator actively opposed revision of the accounting, recordkeeping, enforcement penalties, and administration of the Foreign Corrupt Practices Act (FCPA).

Thus, during the Carter Presidency there was a tenuous balance between trade liberalization and protectionism to combat "unfair" competition. With growing frequency, members of Congress spoke not of free trade but of "fair trade." There was an emerging consensus that Congress should remove export disencentives* and increase incentives for U.S. exporters.

The 97th Congress and the Reagan Administration

To date, neither the international trade bureaucracy nor President Reagan's new Cabinet Council on Economic Affairs has produced a comprehensive trade policy statement. To be sure, the administration has testified before many Congressional trade committees. Regarding trade issues largely removed from domestic economic policy, both Secretary Baldridge and Ambassador Brock have supported Congressional initiatives to eliminate export disincentives. These include strong support for amending the FCPA, further reducing taxation for Americans living overseas, and (prior to the sale of AWACS to Saudi Arabia) considering amendments to the anti-boycott statutes. Support for export incentives, particularly the

---

* Disincentives commonly include human rights export restrictions (especially foreign military sales) ; nuclear equipment or other export controls, particularly for high-technology products; the antitrust laws; restrictions on the export of hazardous goods; the antiboycott statutes; and the FCPA.

Export Trading Company Act of 1981 (S.734), was generated by the Department of Commerce.

In contrast to the policy of the previous administration, President Reagan has opposed certain "subsidies" to business, including expanded funding for the Export-Import Bank loan guarantee program. This same approach looks with disfavor on expanding the Domestic International Sales Corporation, which permits tax deferral of export-related income. As part of the general reduction in the size of the federal bureaucracy, the President's first budget slashed $174 million in funding for the Department of Commerce. The Office of Management and Budget proposed to eliminate the Office of Export Development and the Foreign Commercial Service.

During the first months of the Reagan presidency, many observers of U.S. trade policy expected administration endorsement for creation of a new Department of International Trade and Investment. Originally drafted by Senators Roth and Ribicoff in the 94th Congress, a new version was introduced by Senator Roth, who became chairman of the Senate Committee on Governmental Affairs, which has jurisdiction over all reorganization proposals. Both the supporters and the many detractors of a single agency of international trade saw hearings on the bill as a vehicle to examine reforms for both the organization and conduct of trade policy. Already pledged to abolish two cabinet-level departments, Energy and Education, White House support for a trade department built on a restructured Department of Commerce did not materialize.

Administration opposition to human rights restrictions on exports resulted in the lifting of restraints on sales to Chile and Argentina. Iraq was graduated from the ranks of states supporting international terrorism, and the sale of commercial aircraft was approved. While Presidential spokesmen referred to the simplification and the timely issuance of export licenses, new initiatives were undertaken and managed by the departments of Defense and Commerce to further restrict the sale of militarily significant goods and technologies to the Soviet Union and the COMECON Bloc.* Where Carter administration

---

* The related issues of export controls, high technology, and the American position in COCOM (an informal Coordinating Committee of NATO countries, minus Iceland and Spain plus Japan, which issues guidelines to member governments on national security export controls), and controls on "sensitive" research within the United States, are not examined herein.

147

policy had been erratic, the new administration embarked on a fundamentally new course in export control policy, turning away from restricting specific products and toward control of technologies and production processes, which could enhance the industrial potential of adversaries of the United States.

Emergence of Reciprocity Legislation

When Ronald Reagan took office, Congress was enmeshed in the problem of restricting auto imports. At the same time, many members of Congress and key committees saw increasing competitive challenges to the two categories of exports where America's competitive position was both sound and vigorous: high technology and services.*

For both industries, a major concern is the timeliness with which the federal government is able to respond to "unfair" foreign trade practices. In many instances, federal investigatory and adjudicatory agencies reached final determinations to grant import relief after foreign competitors had either irreparably injured a domestic industry or secured a commanding share of the U.S. market. A new trade policy instrument for high-technology and service exports required a mechanism unencumbered by the complex procedures and apparent delays of the import relief laws.†

Another factor contributing to the evolution of reciprocity legislation was a general dissatisfaction in Congress with the results of the MTN.‡ An attitude more prevalent in the Senate than the House is that the Tokyo Round has not achieved the trade liberalization and

---

* U.S. House of Representatives, Committee on Ways and Means, Subcommittee on Trade, *High Technology and Japanese Industrial Policy: A Strategy for U.S. Policymakers*, Committee Print 96-74 (Washington: GPO, 1980).

† The negative determination by the International Trade Commission in 1979 in the Japanese auto import case reinforced Congressional interest in a new device to react against substantial foreign penetration of U.S. markets. That Japan now has nearly 70 percent of the U.S. market for 64K RAM chips illustrates, for some in Congress, the bankruptcy of the trade laws.

‡ Congressional Budget Office, *U.S. Trade Policy and the Tokyo Round of Multilateral Trade Negotiations*, March 1979 (indicated insubstantial economic benefits of the United States); *The Effects of the Tokyo Round of Multilateral Trade Negotiations on the U.S. Economy: an Updated View*, July 1979 (indicated modest economic benefits of the United States).

the access to foreign markets envisioned at the enactment of the 1979 Trade Agreements Act.

In the months prior to Republican control of the Senate, the Committee on Finance nearly approved a reciprocity bill—also known as mirror-image legislation—regarding a dispute with the Canadians over a tax law which denies a deduction to Canadian advertisers who broadcast on U.S. television stations which reach a Canadian audience. This problem is still before the 97th Congress.*

The Trade Act of 1974 provides the basis for reciprocity legislation. It specifically permits the United States to retaliate unilaterally against foreign trade practices it determines to be unfair. Section 301 recognizes the "multitude of practices" which discriminate against U.S. exports. The Senate Finance Committee, according to its Report on the Trade Act,

> does not intend the "retaliation authority" to be a dead letter. Foreign trading partners should know that we are willing to do business with them on a fair and free basis, but if they insist on maintaining unfair advantages, swift and certain retaliation against their commerce will occur.

To emphasize its determination that the President have a virtually free hand under Section 301, the committee said: "The President ought to be able to act or threaten to act . . . whether or not such action would be entirely consistent with the General Agreement on Tariffs and Trade," an "outmoded" agreement "observed more often in the breach to the detriment of the United States."

The Senate report, considered the most authoritative interpretation of the legislative intent of the Act, permitted the President "to act on either a nondiscriminatory Most Favored Nation or selective basis." Encouraging the use of selective retaliation, the committee "felt it would be unfair to subject innocent foreign countries to retaliatory actions under Section 301. . . ." Finally, Section 301 is explicit that its scope is meant to include service industries in addition to the merchandise sector. Draft legislation pending in Congress may give this legislative history contemporary significance.

* S. 2051 (Danforth—R, Missouri) and H.R. 5205 (Conable—R, N.Y.) These are identical bills to amend the Internal Revenue Code to deny a tax deduction for advertisements on a foreign radio or television station whose market includes the United States if the foreign country denies its advertisers a business deduction for advertisements placed with a U.S. station and directed to a market in that country.

Reciprocity Legislation

Traditionally, reciprocity has meant that the totality of U.S. trade concessions to increase imports would be matched by an equivalent dollar amount of concessions by foreign governments to increase opportunities for U.S. exports. Trade negotiations since the repudiation of Smoot-Hawley in 1934 have never sought to obtain balanced reciprocal concessions product by product or sector by sector. In fact, during the Tokyo Round certain industries contended that their loss of tariff, or nontariff barrier, protection was negotiated away to secure export opportunities for other U.S. industries.

As a class, the reciprocity bills attempt to take into account levels of foreign trade barriers to U.S. exports. Most of the legislation regarding high technology and service exports, and foreign investment issues, provides for unilateral U.S. action without regard to the GATT or MTN dispute settlement procedures. Most proposals do not address the issue that determinations regarding unfairness, subsidization, discrimination, or degree of U.S. access to foreign markets would still be made by the President or regulatory agencies. In other instances the President would be required to implement the recommendations of the International Trade Commission, which ostensibly (due to a high degree of Congressional control) reflects prevailing trends in Congress. Considering often-voiced criticisms of the complexities of the interagency process and the interminable delays that result from agencies of the trade bureaucracy reviewing recommendations prior to their submission to the President, other reciprocity bills create new interagency committees to recommend a course of action in response to alleged unfair foreign trade practices. To date (May 1982) not a single international trade bill cited in this and following sections has become law.

Reciprocity Legislation in the Senate*

1. *S. 898* The Telecommunications Competition and Deregulation Act of 1981
   Committee on Commerce, Science and Transportation
   Sen. Packwood

* The format will include the bill number, title, committee or referral, and chief sponsor.

2. *S. 2051** Deny the Deduction for Certain Advertisements Carried by Certain Foreign Broadcasting Undertakings
   Committee on Finance
   Sen. Danforth

3. *S. 2057* Amendment to Title 49 of the U.S. Code Regarding Licensing of U.S. Commercial Trucks in Canada and Mexico
   Committee on Commerce, Science, and Transportation
   Sen. Kasten

4. *S. 2058* Trade in Services Act of 1982
   Committee on Finance
   Sen. Roth
   (identical bill: H.R. 5457, Sen. Broadhead)

5. *S. 2067* Amends Trade Act of 1974 to Respond to Foreign Practices Which Unfairly Discriminate Against U.S. Investment Abroad
   Committee on Finance
   Sen. Symms
   (identical bill: H.R. 4407, Sen. Schulze)

6. *S. 2071* The Reciprocal Trade Services and Investment Act of 1982
   Committee on Finance
   Sen. Heinz

7. *S. 2094* The Reciprocal Trade and Investment Act of 1982
   Committee on Finance
   Sen. Danforth et al. (twenty cosponsors)

8. *S. 2283* The High Technology Trade Negotiations Act of 1982
   Committee on Finance
   Sen. Glenn

Reciprocity Legislation in the House

1. *H.R. 3037* The Import Relief Improvements Act of 1981
   Committee on Ways and Means, Trade Subcommittee
   Rep. Rinaldo

* See earlier footnote regarding Canadian broadcasting issue. Identical to H.R. 5205, Conable.

2. *H.R. 5158* Telecommunications Act of 1981
   Committee on Energy and Commerce, Subcommittee on Telecommunications, Consumer Protection and Finance
   Rep. Wirth

3. *H.R. 5383* The Trade in Services Act of 1982
   Committees on Foreign Affairs, Energy and Commerce, Judiciary, Ways and Means
   Rep. Gibbons

4. *H.R. 5514* This bill, which has no formal title, provides for retaliation against nontariff barriers
   Committee on Ways and Means
   Rep. Dingell

5. *H.R. 5519* Service Industries Development Act of 1982
   Committees on Ways and Means, Foreign Affairs, and Energy and Commerce
   Rep. Florio et al.

6. *H.R. 5579* The High Technology Trade Act of 1982
   Committees on Foreign Affairs, Ways and Means, Energy and Commerce, Judiciary
   Rep. Gibbons et al.

7. *H.R. 5596* The Trade and Investment Equity Act of 1982
   Committee on Ways and Means
   Rep. Frenzel et al. (thirty-two cosponsors)

8. *H.R. 5614* The Fair Trade with Japan Act
   Committee on Ways and Means
   Rep. Richmond

9. *H.R. 5727* Amendment to the Trade Act
   Rep. Gaydos

Arguments Against Reciprocity Legislation

1. While the United States has consistently preserved in international agreements its right to take unilateral action to restrict imports, the modern history of U.S. trade negotiations has favored a multilateral solution to the resolution of trade disputes. Reciprocity, as a legislative instrument, could seriously undermine the founda-

tions of an already fragile trading system and possibly restrict export markets for U.S. goods and services.

2. Under the provisions of the GATT, foreign countries subjected to unilateral trade restrictions by another country may retaliate by withdrawing trade concessions and restricting the exports of the country which acted unilaterally.

3. Reciprocity by definition implies selective retaliation and a departure from the principles of nondiscrimination and Most Favored Nation treatment in international trade. (In the case of a single imported product, it is often difficult to determine what quantity of products from one country resulted in injury to a domestic industry.)

4. A sectoral or product-oriented approach to reciprocity would be difficult to administer. Should the President decide on retaliation against a foreign trade practice, he would have to select specific items within a product category. Further complicating the situation is the fact that centers of production for many products can be transferred to other countries and restricted goods could be composed of components from several countries, including those not subject to import restrictions.

5. Reciprocity legislation would create a new avenue by which domestic industries could seek protectionist import restraints against foreign competitors.

6. Similarly, reciprocity injects a new dimension into the administration of U.S. trade law. It would require extremely complex political determinations and economic evaluations to quantify the nontariff barriers maintained by other countries against U.S. exports and foreign direct investment.

7. Many of the reciprocity bills stipulate that U.S. retaliation against unfair foreign trade practices depends upon an affirmative determination under section 301 of the Trade Act of 1974. The historical record shows that United States Presidents, from both political parties, have shown great reluctance to use section 301 authority (only one Presidential "recommendation" for retaliation has been made in twenty-six cases).

8. A number of the reciprocity bills call for U.S. negotiators to press for new bilateral and multilateral trade agreements to liberalize trade and reduce trade barriers in high technology, services, and foreign investment. A senior U.S. trade official said such objectives may require a decade of multilateral negotiations.

153

Arguments for Reciprocity Legislation

1. As a result of trade negotiations in the 1970s, the United States substantially reduced tariff and nontariff barriers. Consequently, there are few trade concessions which the United States can offer in exchange for other countries reducing their trade barriers.

2. The threat of restricted access to the U.S. market would compel foreign countries to negotiate seriously to reduce trade barriers. The objective is not to obtain special treatment for U.S. exports, but to obtain export opportunities substantially equivalent to those afforded foreign competitors in the U.S. market.

3. Reciprocity legislation does not do violence to the principles of the GATT. The accepted rules of international trade contained in the GATT do not address restrictions on foreign direct investment, trade in services, or trade relations between Western states and the USSR or the PRC.

4. Proponents maintain that existing U.S. trade laws are inadequate to meet the competitive challenges posed by Japan and other countries which marshal national resources to achieve a commanding export share of foreign markets.

5. MFN principles are not sacrosanct. The EC and several of the MTN codes depart from MFN treatment.

Service Industry Legislation in the 97th Congress

Within the administration, and on Capitol Hill, there is a division of opinion regarding the relationship between reciprocity legislation and proposals to reduce foreign trade barriers to service sector exports. Certain members of Congress who, on principle, oppose reciprocity legislation favor passage of legislation authorizing the President to begin an international negotiation on government policies which distort trade in services. The U.S. government has already compiled a comprehensive list of such barriers.* However, the two major bills on service industries and international trade, while identi-

---

* *U.S. Service Industries in World Markets* (Department of Commerce, 1976; update published in March 1980 by USTR); *Current Developments in U.S. International Service Industries* (Department of Commerce, International Services Division, 1980).

fying negotiating objectives, do not identify specific policies to enhance either the domestic or international competitive position of any U.S. service industry:

1. *S. 1233* The Service Industries Development Act
   Committee on Commerce, Science and Transportation
   Sen. Inouye et al.

2. *H.R. 1957* International Communications Reorganization Act of 1981
   Committees on Government Operations, Foreign Affairs
   Rep. English et al.

Other Trade Policy Issues in Legislative Format Before the 97th Congress

A U.S. Department of International Trade

1. *S. 1493* Department of Commerce, Trade, and Technology. Organization Act (*a bill from the 96th Congress*)
   Sen. Stevenson

2. *S. 970* International Trade and Investment Reorganization Act of 1981
   Committee on Governmental Affairs
   Sen. Roth et al.

This legislation terminates the Department of Commerce and the USTR. It establishes a new department to include the Customs Service, the Export-Import Bank, the Overseas Private Investment Corporation, functions of USTR, and trade functions of Commerce, Treasury, and State. It transfers from the Department of Commerce to other agencies non-trade-related offices and establishes an independent Bureau of the Census.

Its mission would include the protection of American industry, labor, and agriculture from injurious or unfair foreign competition; the assessment of foreign trade practices; and responsibility for an import monitoring system. (The Trade Act of 1974 called for the President to establish such a system, but the proposal was not implemented by the executive branch because of apprehension that it would provide the basis for protectionist requests.)

Comprehensive Trade Bills

1. *S. 930* The National Export Policy Act
   Committee on Banking, Housing and Urban Affairs
   Sen. Roth et al. (twelve cosponsors)
2. *H.R. 3173* The National Export Policy Act of 1981
   Committees on Agriculture; Banking, Finance and Urban Affairs; Foreign Affairs; Energy and Commerce; Judiciary; Small Business; Ways and Means
   Rep. AuCoin et al. (twenty-seven cosponsors)

Both of these bills were assembled by the Senate and House Export Caucuses. The objective is to stimulate Congressional discussion of trade policy issues, which include export credit financing; taxation of U.S. citizens living overseas; establishing Export Trading Companies; weakening the enforcement standards of the Foreign Corrupt Practices Act; promoting and financing agricultural exports; initiating international negotiations regarding subsidized export credits, services, reciprocity in antitrust enforcement; export promotion (with special reference for small business); and liberalization of tax provisions regarding export-related income and other expenses involved in exporting.

Export Trading Companies

Legislation to create a statutory basis for Export Trading Companies is based on the premise that small and medium-sized firms need special assistance with the technical aspects of exports, financing, risk coverage, foreign market research, and overseas sales. The Department of Commerce estimates that of 250,000 manufacturing concerns in the United States, less than 10,000 are engaged in the export trade and less than 2,000 account for 85 percent of all U.S. exports.

The various ETC bills now in Congress contain, in not quite the same form, four basic provisions: (1) Banking—to permit banks and bank holding companies to assume an equity position in ETC;

(2) Antitrust—to provide an exemption from the antitrust laws through a special certification process and extend this exemption to service industries; (3) Financing—to use federal funds to meet the financing needs of small and medium-sized firms; (4) Tax—to extend the DISC provisions for deferral of taxes on export income to ETC and to include certain banking organizations.

There are currently five major ETC bills before the House:

1. H.R. 1648—Rep. LaFalce (identical to S. 734)
2. H.R. 1799—Rep. Bonker
3. H.R. 2123—Rep. Gibbons
4. H.R. 2851—Rep. Patterson
5. H.R. 2326—Rep. Rodino

Foreign Corrupt Practices Act

1. *S. 708* Business Accounting and Foreign Trade Simplification Act
   Committee on Banking, Housing and Urban Affairs
   Sen. Chafee et al.

2. *H.R. 2530* Business Accounting and Foreign Trade Simplification Act (identical to the Senate bill, but no action taken by the House)
   Rep. Rinaldo et al.

This legislation is an example of differences between the Senate and the House regarding the removal of export disincentives. It also demonstrates the power of a subcommittee chairman with jurisdiction over the legislation to prevent consideration by the House. The administration strongly favors amending FCPA provisions concerning corporate recordkeeping, internal accounting controls, and the criminalization of foreign bribery.

Export-Import Bank

Widespread Congressional dissatisfaction with the effectiveness of the "Gentlemen's Agreement" among the industrialized allies to restrict the use of export credit subsidies resulted in proposals to establish a "war chest" that would enable the Export-Import Bank to counteract foreign subsidized export credits:

1. *S. 868* Competitive Export Financing Act of 1981
   Committee on Banking, Housing and Urban Affairs
   Sen. Heinz et al.

2. *H.R. 3228* Competitive Export Subsidy Fund Act
   Committee on Banking, Finance and Urban Affairs
   Rep. Neal et al.

Antitrust

1. *S. 432* To Establish a Commission on the International Application of the Antitrust Laws (identical bill: H.R. 2459, Rep. McClory)
   Committee on the Judiciary
   Sen. Mathias et al.

This proposal (formerly S. 1010 in the 96th Congress and reported favorably to the Senate, Senate Report No. 96-770) would initiate a one-year study and make recommendations to the President on the antitrust laws, court rules, administrative procedures, and extra-territorial application of the antitrust laws. The administration opposes this bill.

2. *S. 1968* International Joint Venture Act of 1981
   Committee on the Judiciary
   Sen. Hatch et al.

Export Controls

The issues regarding the effects on U.S. national security of the transfer of sensitive technologies to the Soviet Union and other communist countries should be reflected in a number of new legislative proposals. The implications of changing the decision-making process by which export licenses are granted (including shifting responsibility to the Department of Defense from the Department of Commerce) and the ability of U.S. high-technology companies to market their products overseas will be the subject of several hearings by Senate and House committees with jurisdiction over the Export Administration Act of 1979, which expires on September 30, 1983. The existing statute, according to several studies, does not adequately address reducing the paperwork burden on potential exporters; accelerating the process of approving or denying export license applications; identifying domestic exporters and foreign consignees likely to ship controlled goods and technologies to communist and other proscribed countries; clarifying the use of foreign policy controls (i.e., the grain embargo); and improving enforcement capabilities to interdict nonlicensed high-technology sales.

The following legislation indicates the beginnings of an intense Congressional debate over the reauthorization of the Export Administration Act.

1. *H.R. 513* A bill to Amend the Export Administration Act of 1979
   Committee on Armed Services and Foreign Affairs
   Rep. Roe

2. *H.R. 4590* Technology Transfer Control Act of 1981
   Committee on Foreign Affairs
   Rep. Dornan

3. *S. 2606* (96th Congress) The Office of Strategic Trade Act
   Committee on Banking
   Sen. Garn

Other export control issues involve the export of hazardous wastes (S. 622, Sen. Inouye); the export of goods which are prohibited or restricted in the United States (H.R. 2439, Rep. Barnes), and the denial of certain export licenses and restrictions on the imports of countries which aid and abet international terrorism (S. 635, Sen. Heinz, the Antiterrorism Act).

PART B: INDUSTRIAL POLICY AND INTERNATIONAL TRADE

Beginning with the Carter administration, public policy officials in Congress and the executive branch made increasing reference to the absence of a formal U.S. industrial policy, i.e., those actions of the federal government which directly or indirectly favor one industry over another. Reindustrialization, revitalization, and economic renewal became the titles of economic recovery programs advanced by

Amitai Etzione, President Carter, and President Reagan, respectively. Advocates of "targeting," picking winners over losers, or advocates of the diversion of federal resources to invigorate ailing basic industries (through a modern version of a Reconstruction Finance Corporation or a National Development Bank) are in effect advocating an American industrial policy.

Developing and implementing an industrial policy would probably require a program-by-program evaluation to establish priorities for further action among federal laws, programs, and regulations which affect the following: capital formation, industrial innovation, productivity, government-business-labor relations, patent policy, federal credits, loans and loan guarantees for business, job training and education programs, and federal procurement policies.*

What follows is a survey of federal programs which have a relationship with U.S. trade performance and which are therefore components of an implicit federal industrial policy. Enhancing U.S. international competitiveness is a goal identified by constituencies supporting expansion of existing programs.

Federal Business Credit Programs

1. The Regular Business Loan Program (section 7a) of the Small Business Administration.

The program tends to direct the majority of loans to service industries, especially in the wholesale and retail trade, as opposed to manufacturing concerns.

2. The Business Development Assistance Program of the Economic Development Administration (EDA), including the Special Steel Loan Guarantee Program.

EDA's legislative mandate requires that it target its financial resources toward regions with significant unemployment and regional development problems. Its loans are largely directed toward manufacturing enterprises. EDA also administers the *Trade Adjustment Assistance Program* for industries which have been injured by im-

* Robert B. Reich, "Making Industrial Policy," *Foreign Affairs*, Spring 1982, pp. 852–881. The views of a former FTC official on the need for positive adjustment policies.

port competition (mostly the footwear, apparel, textile, and cutlery industries). The steel program is designed to assist companies to modernize their production facilities, increase productivity, and reduce costs, in part to remain competitive with foreign imports.

In an economy moving away from manufacturing and toward services, a basic policy issue is whether federal programs diverting credit toward manufacturing would distort U.S. economic development.

Federal Credit Activities

Although 1982 was not the year for legislative action, the Congress was apprehensive regarding the economic effects of "off-budget" loan guarantee programs. During the 96th Congress, several bills addressed this issue by proposing comprehensive credit control procedures (major examples are H.R. 5683, the Federal Credit Program Control Act of 1979, and S. 2151, introduced by Senator Percy). Examples of "off-budget" direct loan and loan guarantee programs include:

- Export-Import Bank
- Commodity Credit Corporation
- Small Business Administration
- Economic Development Administration
- Foreign Military Credit Sales
- Overseas Private Investment Corporation
- Chrysler and Lockheed Loan Guarantee Programs

An argument could be made that the most significant federal industrial policy since World War II has been the rapid expansion of off-budgetary loan and loan guarantee authority. In fiscal 1981, the federal credit budget was in excess of $140 billion, or approximately one-quarter the size of the unified federal budget. The effects are massive federal subsidies to selected groups. Total loans outstanding exceed $500 billion, the effects of which on economic indicators have not been examined.*

---

* Congressional Budget Office, *Federal Credit Activities: an Analysis of the President's Credit Budget of 1981*, Staff Working Paper (Washington: GPO, 1980).

Technological Innovation

In October 1979, President Carter submitted to Congress a message containing a number of initiatives designed to ensure that the United States would remain "the world leader in industrial innovation." The report was the result of an extensive Domestic Policy Review (DPR) on Industrial Innovation which addressed the following issues:

- Increasing technical knowledge
- Improving and modernizing the patent system
- Clarifying antitrust policy
- Enhancing the development of small business (considered to be the most innovative segment)
- Adjusting federal procurement to encourage innovations
- Federal assistance to facilitate labor/business adjustment to innovation

The Economic Revitalization Proposal that followed contained tax and other economic measures to complement the DPR. These measures included liberalized depreciation, a refundable tax credit, tax incentives for small business, targeted tax credits for distressed areas, and increased federal spending to support basic research.

The DPR and statements by the Reagan administration during the debate on the 1981 Economic Recovery Act presume an integral relationship between the level of R&D spending and the level of success in international competitiveness.

Legislation Pertaining to Industrial Innovation

1. *P.L. 96-480* (S. 1250) Stevenson-Wydler Technology Innovation Act of 1980 (a bill enacted by the 96th Congress)
   Sen. Stevenson

This establishes within the Department of Commerce an Office of Industrial Technology to study technology-related issues, including "the world trade performance of the United States and foreign industrial sectors," and to make recommendations to the President and Congress. (The Reagan administration has not authorized the expenditure of funds to comply with the Act.)

Tax Incentives

1. *P.L. 97-34 (H.R. 4242)* The Economic Recovery Act of 1981

This provides for a 25 percent tax credit for additional R&D expenditures over a specified base period and an additional 25 percent tax credit on 65 percent of all corporate payments to universities to perform basic research.

It revised the procedures for determining depreciation schedules by incorporating the 10-5-3 Capital Cost Recovery Act for structures, equipment, and vehicles. Other provisions reduced the effective overall rate of taxation on business and investment income.*

(Following passage of H.R. 4242, a number of Congressional Democrats proposed that legislation be enacted to amend the budget process to include tax measures which result in a loss of revenue to the Treasury. Such legislation would in their view discipline the tax-writing committees by setting a ceiling on tax expenditures (S. 2069, Sen. Hart, and H.R. 4882, Rep. Bonior).

Patents

1. *H.R. 4564* The Uniform Federal Research and Development Utilization Act of 1981
   Committees on Judiciary, and on Science and Technology
   Rep. Ertel

This establishes a uniform federal patent system for the protection and promotion of the results of federally sponsored R&D in science and technology.

2. *S. 255* Patent Term Restoration Act of 1981 (H.R. 1937, Rep. Kastenmeier, identical bill)
   Sen. Mathias et al.

This legislation extends the length of a patent to include the time required by a company to obtain approval from certain federal regulatory agencies to market the patented product.

---

* General Accounting Office, *An Analytical Framework for Federal Policies and Programs Influencing Capital Formation in the United States*, Report Number PAD-80-24 (Washington: GAO, 1980).

3. *S. 1957* The Uniform Science and Technology Research and Development Utilization Act
   Committee on Commerce, Science and Transportation
   Sen. Schmitt

This provides for a uniform patent system regarding federally sponsored R&D in science and technology.

Small Business

1. *H.R. 4326* The Small Business Innovation Development Act (related bill: S. 851, Sen. Rudman, passed Senate 90 to 0 on 12/8/81, Report No. 97-194)
   Committees on Energy and Commerce, Armed Services, Science and Technology, Small Business, Veterans' Affairs, Intelligence, Foreign Affairs
   Rep. La Folce et al.

This legislation requires federal agencies which engage in R&D funding to establish Small Business Innovation Research Programs to be funded by a mandatory set-aside (19 percent), thus increasing participation by small businesses in federally sponsored R&D.

Merger Policy

Another element of de facto industrial policy is federal policy regarding mergers and acquisitions. The regulatory agencies involved include the Federal Trade Commission, the Securities and Exchange Commission, and the Antitrust Division of the Department of Justice.

Recent and substantial acquisitions in the energy industry have focused attention on merger issues. In the absence of new legislation, the federal courts continue to apply a strict standard to the enforcement of the antitrust laws. Congress has not attempted to identify or establish new enforcement standards which take into account the interests of shareholders or communities, the effects on industrial innovation, or federal policy objectives to promote industrial or regional development.

Organization for Science and Technology

The National Science and Technology Policy, Organization, and Priorities Act of 1976 (P.L. 94-282) requires the National Science Foundation to report annually to Congress on domestic science and technology issues. The statute also charged NSF with responsibility for developing and making recommendations for long-term science and technology planning. This mandate has not been fulfilled. Neither the Congressional Office of Technology Assessment nor the White House Office of Science and Technology Policy (OSTP) has presented a comprehensive set of recommendations to Congress. The decentralized character of science policy and the absence of a comprehensive working budget that includes all federal science programs and expenditures for R&D inhibit long-range planning.

1. *H.R. 2640* (96th Congress) National Science and Technology Corporation Act (Related bill: H.R. 8181, Rep. Ottinger, to create a National Industrial Innovation Corporation)
   Committees on Science and Technology, Banking and Rules
   Rep. Downey

This legislation establishes a National Science and Technology Corporation with the authority to guarantee loans to promote private sector R&D and to encourage the commercialization of federally developed technologies.

2. *H.R. 3137* Information Science and Technology Act of 1981
   Committee on Science and Technology
   Rep. Brown, G.

This creates an Institute for Information Policy and Research to develop, in part, policy options for the management of federal R&D.

3. *H.R. 3749* National Technology Foundation Act of 1981
   Committees on Science and Technology, and Judiciary
   Rep. Brown, G., et al.

This establishes the National Technology Foundation as an independent agency to promote the advancement of technology and to study the relationship between technology and U.S. international trade performance.

4. *H.R. 1908* Research and Development Authorization Estimates Act
   Committee on Science and Technology
   Rep. Fuqua

This amends the Presidential Science and Technology Advisory Organization Act to establish a multiyear plan for all federal R&D expenditures.

FINANCING THE FUTURE

Federal funding, whether direct through appropriations or indirect through tax incentives, is a common thread that links de facto industrial policies. A national industrial policy will require significant federal funding, credit guarantees, and tax expenditures. However, in its present form the Congressional budget process does not allow for the establishment and adjustment of spending priorities to achieve specific policy objectives. For example, the appropriations committees in Congress, and the respective committees that authorize actual program expenditures, do not have a mechanism to evaluate the importance of one program against another in related sections of the budget. Also, to date there has been no comprehensive review of federal R&D expenditures to determine which programs, and at what funding levels, will achieve the Congressionally mandated objectives that necessitated expenditures in the first place.

A major constraint on the budget process is the allocation of funding on the basis of one fiscal year. Some observers of the budget process recommend multiyear funding. This mechanism might afford Congress the opportunity to exercise its policy oversight responsibilities in order to evaluate program expenditures. Multiyear funding and comprehensive program reviews might also tend to insulate members of Congress from the annual appeals of domestic political constituencies that favor particular programs. Should the United States choose to "revitalize" industries such as the steel industry, cost becomes the only impediment. Tax incentives linked to specific types of expenditures could lead to an industry's long-term viability.

Because of Congressional, executive branch, and private-sector resistance to the notion of industrial policy modeled after the Japanese or Western Europeans, the budget process could become a powerful tool to direct federal programs to enhance the competitiveness of certain industrial sectors.

New industrial policies, divorced from existing programs that already benefit one industry, may emerge first from the executive branch. Sustained by virtually unlimited funding, the Department of Defense is seeking to develop new technologies and also is seeking control over their development and applications. One example is its Very-High-Speed Integrated Circuit (VHSIC) program.

Whether or not justified as enhancing U.S. international competitiveness, an industrial policy will require a vision for the future and the political will to "reform" existing federal programs before proposing and implementing a legislative agenda. The Japanese already have published a vision for their industrial future which outlines a series of strategic goals. An American version of Japan's vision spelled out by its Ministry of International Trade and Industry would at best be an academic exercise without any foundation in politically possible public policy. To articulate goals for the future necessitates specific reference to existing policies. The now hollow shell of free trade ideology, rising protectionism, and apprehension of foreign industries supported financially by their governments tends to solidify political support for present policies.

A new direction for international trade policy, and the modification of existing domestic economic programs that now assist certain industries, will be a long-term process requiring strong leadership by the President, by his chief cabinet officers, key Congressional leadership, and business leaders.

Before planning for the future we need evaluation of today's federal policies that shape our industrial outlook. This is the prerequisite for a vision of the future and an accompanying political agenda. A working document of present policies, and what led to their status in the law, is by its very nature a spark to ignite high political drama.

Even conducting a detailed look at the present will require assigning a cabinet officer the authority and responsibility to direct the effort.

"The changing policies of other governments and the changing methods of regulating international trade greatly complicate the Government's task of proper direction of American trade." In 1933

167

Franklin Roosevelt further observed that "under the Administration's program the numerous recovery departments are assigned powers and or duties which directly impact upon trade relations with other countries." Roosevelt saw the connection between "industrial policy" and trade policy. A half-century later we have yet to organize the government to act based upon this connection.

Technological Innovation and Industrial Competition: Fostering the American Entrepreneurial Spirit

William J. Perry

Introduction

Each year in April, the investment firm of Hambrecht & Quist holds a technology conference in which presidents of more than a hundred high-technology companies describe their companies to a group of potential investors. This year, there were nearly a thousand investors from all over the world, representing in aggregate an investment potential of many tens of billions of dollars. Several hundred of these investors were from Western Europe, and as I talked with them, I asked them why they were interested in investing in U.S. companies. During the four years I was in the Defense Department, I visited many industrial companies in Western Europe and learned firsthand of the very impressive technology in those countries. So, I wondered, why would the institutional investors in Europe invest in American high-technology companies? The answer, of course, is that while the technology level in Europe is very high, it is concentrated almost entirely in large companies—high-technology *ventures* are almost nonexistent. There is no counterpart in Western Europe to our Silicon Valley, in which hundreds of start-up companies are introducing new technology and new products to the world. The United States not only has leadership in technology—a leadership which is being challenged—but it has undisputed leadership in the innovative technology stemming from new ventures.

Since the benefits of this leadership are significant, I have been led to ask, "What are the factors that produced this leadership in the United States? And what do we have to do to sustain our leadership position?" If we understand how we achieved this leadership, maybe we can get a better understanding of what it will take to keep it. In considering this question, I looked for root causes of technological leadership in the United States—economic, educational, and cultural.

The American Tradition of Innovation

The cultural factors are hardest to evaluate. I believe that the tradition of technical inventions in the United States runs very deep. It goes back to colonial days, and was pronounced in the early history of the Republic. One of our heroes, of course, is Benjamin Franklin, who, even though he was living in what was then a backward country, probably was the most prominent inventor of his day. His inventions are typical of what came to be called Yankee ingenuity: we were not as scientifically advanced as the European countries, but we had a predisposition to invent practical things that had commercial application. During the nineteenth century, the United States led the world in inventions to further agriculture: the cotton gin, the reaper, the harvester, and the steamboat were typical of what I would call the first phase of technological innovation in America.

The second phase began with Edison. Edison, it seems to me, was quite different from any of his predecessors. He was the precursor of the modern technologist. He not only invented devices which even today have important applications—the electric light, the phonograph, and (almost) the vacuum tube (one of his great regrets was that he just missed the vacuum tube invention)—but even more importantly, he *invented a way of inventing*. He can, I think, properly be credited with inventing the modern R&D laboratory where a team of technically trained people systematically explores ways of applying science and technology to practical devices with commercial value.

The third phase in our history of technological innovation was precipitated by three catalytic events which happened over a fifteen-year period. During the mid-1930s, a wave of refugees came into this country as a result of Hitler's persecution of Jews and intellectuals in central Europe. Refugees were nothing new to the United States, but this group of refugees included some of the world's most capable scientists and engineers, who, when added to our native scientists and engineers, created a "critical mass" of technical talent in the United States. Then, during the Second World War, the government made a massive investment in R&D at laboratories like the Radiation Laboratory at MIT and the Radio Research Laboratory at Harvard. That was something new on the American scene; Edison "invented" the R&D laboratory, but this was the first time that his invention was applied on a massive scale and with government funding. That became a tradition that has been maintained in this country ever since, although today defense R&D is accomplished primarily in private industry rather than in government laboratories. Then, after the war, this group of European scientists and engineers and the newly trained American scientists and engineers fresh from their experience in the R&D laboratories in the Second World War went back to universities to train a whole new generation going to school under the GI Bill. When that new generation of technical talent started flowing into our industries in the mid-1950s and the 1960s, they created, among other things, the microelectronics revolution of the 1960s, the most prominent aspect of the third phase of technological innovation in America.

The Coming VLSI Revolution

There is no question that the United States was the world leader of the microelectronics revolution that occurred in the '60s and the early '70s. But today, the U.S. microelectronics industry appears to be running out of steam. With the maturing of large-scale integrated circuit (LSI) technology, we see the leadership shifting to Japan, with a corresponding loss to our own economy. But, as the LSI revolution winds down, the very-large-scale integrated circuits (VLSI) revolution is just getting under way. Indeed, we are at the dawn of a new era. The VLSI revolution, in my judgment, will be more exciting and even more economically significant than was the LSI revolution.

Let me explain briefly what I mean by VLSI and why I use the dramatic term "revolution" to describe what is about to happen. By VLSI, I mean the construction of microelectronic chips at submicron geometries; that is, the construction of chips in which the elements are spaced less than one micron* apart. We are today routinely building chips with about five-micron spacing. VLSI will take us down to about a half-a-micron spacing. Now, a decrease in spacing by a factor of ten in each dimension means that we will be increasing the density by about a factor of a hundred. To put it another way, we will be able to put about a hundred times as many transistors on a chip as we can today; that is, we will be putting more than one million transistors on a chip in the VLSI era. It is difficult to understand the full significance of that by just quoting the numbers. By comparison, if we consider the field of transportation, a hundredfold improvement in speed was effected when we went from the horse and buggy to the jet transport, from about five miles an hour to about five hundred miles an hour. I think it is fair to call a hundredfold improvement a revolutionary change, particularly inasmuch as this change in microelectronics is going to happen over seven or eight years, not in the fifty or more years it took to make the transition to the jet transport.

That change in performance will require revolutionary new processes—we will have to break the "optical barrier." Since the integrated circuit was invented, we have been making evolutionary improvements of it, bringing the transistors closer and closer together by refining the process technology. In all cases, the process technology was based on optical principles, but as we get down to submicron spacings, optical principles will no longer be applicable. We are approaching the wavelength of light when we get below a micron, and therefore the optical systems will no longer provide the resolution needed for lithographic systems used in manufacturing the chips. A brand-new manufacturing process technology will have to be developed in order to carry this revolution forward. So, both in terms of performance and in terms of the kind of process used, the changes will indeed be revolutionary.

It is worth looking, then, at what the impact of those revolutionary changes is likely to be on our industry. To the semiconductor industry itself, this new technology, the new processes, and the new devices will lead to a period of unprecedented change in an industry that is accustomed to change. There will be a new period of growth

* A micron is one millionth of a meter.

172

in the semiconductor industry, and that growth will lead, I believe, to a restructuring of companies in the direction of vertical integration to a much greater extent than we have ever seen in the semiconductor industry in the past. There will also be an introduction of new companies in the semiconductor industry. In the '60s there was a wave of new semiconductor companies, and then a long pause; in the '70s there were almost no new semiconductor companies formed. That has changed; the last few years have seen a new wave of emerging semiconductor companies. Even within the existing companies, there is going to be a reshuffling of leadership, and in fact the companies that are leaders today are going to have a difficult problem fighting against the *disadvantage* of being a leader. Those companies that were the leaders in the development and production of vacuum tubes were conspicuously unsuccessful in making the transition to transistors. Even the companies that succeeded with transistors were not necessarily the leaders in the integrated circuit revolution. As new processes evolve, a company must seize the opportunity and move forward with that new process; and very often leadership in the old process turns out to be a liability instead of an asset. So we should look for leadership changes in the semiconductor industry, and some of these new leaders will be companies whose names are not yet known to the public.

In addition to those changes in the semiconductor industry directly, there will be a profound change in the whole set of industries that revolve around the semiconductor industry—the suppliers of manufacturing equipment, for example. Since the manufacturing equipment is going to be new, different, and expensive, there will be an impetus to build up a whole new manufacturing equipment industry and, indeed, that is already underway.

The change in the computer industry will be especially significant. Until now the computer companies have simply been taking advantage of the improvement in cost performance which they can achieve by using chips with a lower cost per transistor. But when chips become available with a million transistors, there will be opportunities to do something quite different in computer architecture, and those companies able to conceive of changes in architecture which most effectively exploit the VLSI technology will have an advantage over their competition. As a result of these changes in computers, there

173

will be a whole new wave of computer software companies formed, since software will become more and more the dominant factor in efficiency and productivity in the use of computers.

I've talked so far about the semiconductor industry, the computer industry, and the software industry which is associated with it, but the new commercial and industrial products which come out of these industries will proliferate into all aspects of our life. They are already going into our homes in the form of the personal computer, but I believe that we are in about the same position today with the personal computer that we were with the hand-held calculator the year the HP-35 was introduced. A major new industry is ahead of us, and the future is going to dwarf anything that has happened to date. Applications of computers in factories are already under way. We are just scratching the surface of robotic applications today, and since VLSI permits cost-performance advantages of a factor of 100 over present systems, we will see an unfolding of robotics applications that is far more substantial than anything we see today or even can conceive of today. Perhaps even more important than the applications to the factory will be the applications to the office. Most of the gainfully employed workers in the industrial countries today are officeworkers, and the move to increase their productivity will focus around putting microcomputers in each telephone, thereby marrying communication and computing devices.

Finally, an issue of great significance is the application of microelectronics to defense. LSI and VLSI allow the creation of what the Pentagon calls "silver bullets"—the precision-guided munitions which allow a single weapon to make a direct hit on a target the first time it is fired. This will have, and in fact already is having, a revolutionary impact on our defense capability. I have described this application at length in several articles,* so I will not discuss it here.

Maintaining Our Competitive Posture

The burning question, then, in the face of all of these benefits, is whether the United States will be able to maintain the leadership in the VLSI revolution that it has enjoyed in the LSI revolution. In par-

* See, for example, my article in *Technology Review*, July 1982.

ticular, will we be able to compete with Japan? It is instructive to read the analysis that has been made by MITI, the Ministry of International Trade and Industry in Japan. They have made a projection for where their country should be going in the '80s. They have seen the benefits that I have described and have declared that it will be a national policy for Japan to assume world leadership in this VLSI revolution. They have recognized that success in that objective will require a different kind of effort than they have applied in the past; it will require leadership in technological innovation. Technical imitation and production skills will not be sufficient to seize leadership in this new field. They have seen that; they have stated it as a national objective; they have formulated a plan; and they have put the funding forward to try to achieve that objective. It is interesting to compare this with the United States' effort, to estimate which country will win the competition. R&D will be the key. We do not have, and we are not likely to have, any program comparable to MITI's VLSI program; we do not have an organization comparable to MITI; we do not have a national planning activity; nor do we have a way of funding commercially directed R&D on a national basis.

Funding for Research

Notwithstanding that, there are many factors in our favor. First of all, consider the program called VHSIC—the Defense Department's name for VLSI. (It stands for "very-high-speed integrated circuits.") The Defense Department will be investing $300 million to advance VLSI technology in order to make it available for defense systems at an early date. In addition to this, the six companies that are working on the VHSIC program for the Defense Department have plans themselves to invest additional R&D dollars, which in aggregate will mean that about $1 billion will be spent on VLSI development over the next five years.

Industry is also working with universities in this regard. Stanford University has created a Center for Integrated Systems to advance VLSI technology, supported by a consortium of fifteen different industrial firms. Each of the firms has committed $1 million, and that $15 million is going to Stanford to build the facility which will house the Center for Integrated Systems. The Defense Department, through the Advanced Research Project Agency, is investing about $8 million a year to fund the projects at that center. So here is one form of cooperation between university, industry, and the federal government which will advance R&D in this field. At the University of California, a still different approach called the Micro Program is being used. In the Micro Program, individual professors conceive VLSI research programs, which they propose to industry. If industry is willing to put up half the funds, they are assured of getting the other half of the funds for that research from the state. MIT, Cornell, and North Carolina have similar programs all intended to advance VLSI technology.

Initiatives to Foster Technical Education

There is a very real problem in providing the technical talent necessary to sustain this microelectronics revolution that I have been discussing. During the decade of the 1970s, when the electronics industry nearly tripled in size, the number of electrical engineers and computer scientists who were graduated annually in the United States remained essentially constant. That says very clearly that we have been "living off the fat." We had this enormous input of technical talent as a result of the GI Bill, but very many of those graduates are no longer making technical contributions to the industry. They are either retired, "kicked up" to management positions, or working in some other field. The problems stemming from this growing shortage of technical talent will not manifest themselves immediately. Industry is forestalling the immediate effects by hiring the brightest graduates before they go on to graduate school, thereby cutting off the supply of future professors—and they're hiring the professors as well. Hiring the graduates has been described as eating our seed corn; hiring the professors could be described as shooting the farmer. This is a very serious situation, since the infusion of new technical talent into our industries will determine the ability of this country to compete with Japan and Western Europe during the middle to late 1980s.

The federal government is doing little, if anything, about this problem, and it is debatable whether it should. It is quite clear that both the federal and state governments have substantial responsibility for correcting our problems in secondary and primary education. I am not as convinced that the national government has a primary role in providing engineers to industry. I think that there are perhaps better ways of attacking that problem; in particular, I think that industry should be working with the universities to solve this problem. The American Electronics Association has created an Electronic Education Foundation to provide support to the universities. This foundation will be supplementing the salaries of hundreds of EE and computer science professors by an amount on the order of $10,000 to $15,000 a year, and it will be providing graduate fellowships to hundreds of students who intend to become university teachers, since that is the most immediate problem in building up our educational infrastructure. It is encouraging industry to provide new equipment to the universities. Finally, it is developing a program in continuing education to retrain and improve the capabilities of engineers already in industry. The American Electronics Association has asked each of its member companies to allocate 2 percent of their R&D budget to the support of universities. If all of the companies did that, it would represent more than $100 million a year going to universities from the electronics industry alone. This is an ambitious effort, one which requires the support of thousands of smaller companies as well as the larger companies that are already getting organized to provide it. I am fairly optimistic that the program will have real success, but I believe we are fighting an uphill battle—we started much later than we should have, and the problems are already very serious.

Financing for R&D

Let me now turn to the financial climate for innovation. I distinguish between the financial problems of start-up companies and the financial problems of large, established companies, since they are quite different. For start-up companies in the United States, the availability of financing is better today than it has ever been before. Venture money is available as a result of several important developments which have occurred in the last few years. First, and most significant, was the reduction in the capital gains tax rate in 1978 and again in 1981. This has made it very attractive to make high-risk investments if these investments have the potential of making large capital gains. Second, institutional investors are now starting to put some of their funds, including portions of insurance and pen-

177

sion funds, into venture capital because the fund managers are impressed with the performance of venture funds of this past decade. A number of well-known venture funds have achieved growth rates averaging more than 30 percent a year over the past decade. Therefore, funds which traditionally were being invested in "blue chip" stocks such as General Motors or U.S. Steel are now being diverted to high-technology companies—most of it to *large* high-technology companies, but an increasing portion of it to *start-up* companies. Another phenomenon has been R&D partnerships, in which a new company is organized and funded as a partnership instead of a corporation. The advantage from an investor's point of view is that during the start-up phase—the several years during which the company can expect to have only losses—the losses flow through to the partners and can be claimed on their income tax. Therefore, during the loss period investors get a tax benefit, which reduces their risk. Then, if the company succeeds, it will be incorporated and the partnership shares will be exchanged for stock and the investors will have the potential of realizing capital gains from their investment. The R&D partnership has become quite popular for obvious reasons, and it has brought new sources of investment money to new ventures.

The problem of capital formation for the larger high-technology companies is more difficult. Interest rates have been at all-time highs these past few years. Even today, the prime rate is still 5–6 percent higher than the inflation rate—much higher than historical rates. This means that American companies have to either pay too much for needed capital or else forego capital expansion. If this capital expansion continues to be delayed, it will have a deleterious effect on the future of our companies. If we look at the competitive situation, for example in Japan, we find that capital availability is very much better there. The data I have seen suggest that Japanese companies have a fundamental advantage over U.S. companies in availability of relatively cheap long-term capital.

Outlook for the Future

I would like to conclude with a comment on the cultural climate for innovation. I began by alluding to Yankee ingenuity—the tendency of Americans to invent practical things. I think Yankee ingenuity is alive and well in this country. One of the reasons it keeps going, I think, is that we have successful role models all around us who have succeeded as entrepreneurs by using technology to invent useful and practical things. These successful role models play an undefinable but very important role in keeping our inventive spirit going. On the contrary, if you look at Japan, West Germany, or the United Kingdom, the entrepreneurial role models are almost nonexistent. Can you imagine, those of you who have dealt with Mitsubishi or Hitachi or Siemens, the chief engineer of one of those companies "spinning off" and forming his own company? Their culture would recoil at that—it is almost unthinkable. So, for better or for worse, we live in an entrepreneurial climate that allows these new ventures to take seed and grow, and this climate currently is unique to our country.

In sum, the next wave of this postwar technological revolution—the VLSI revolution—is just getting under way. It's going to have the same kind of characteristics that the LSI revolution had in creating new jobs, new products, new ways of doing things, new industries, and new wealth. There is every reason to believe that the United States will be the dominant factor in that revolution just as it was in the LSI revolution, but it is not going to be automatic. The competition, particularly from Japan, will be fierce, and we have important weaknesses in our posture compared with our situation in 1960. One particular problem is in R&D, with the government decreasing its support of research. I think we should try to get the government to turn around on that; it is a very small cost with a very large payoff. We also have a serious weakness in our educational structure; I am most concerned about the failure of our universities to cope with the increased demand for electrical engineers and computer scientists. And we have weakness in our financial structure because of our declining ability to provide low-cost capital to our larger, well-established companies. But we do not have a problem in providing capital to the new technological ventures—we are doing very well in that field. And our inventive spirit is alive and well. If I had to balance all of these, I would say that the factors that are fundamental to our success are positive, and the problems that I can identify all lie within our ability to solve.

179

Policies to Stimulate Growth: The View from a New Industry

Robert A. Swanson

Innovation: A Critical Resource

Biotechnology is one of the high-technology industries that is expected to figure importantly in the future economies of the advanced industrialized nations. This entire industry derives from research breakthroughs in the biological sciences that have been taking place over the last several decades. My company, Genentech, Inc., is dedicated to the application of new tools such as recombinant DNA technology to produce important proteins, including hormones and enzymes, for commercial use. As such, we are an entrepreneurial company in a young industry in which innovation is the basis of our existence and a requirement for future growth.

It is clear that innovation in technology is critical for a vigorous national economy, the creation of new jobs, and the international competitiveness of U.S. industry. Perhaps the experience of Genentech can suggest some general principles that may be helpful in the stimulation of innovation.

My partner in starting Genentech, Dr. Herbert Boyer of the University of California at San Francisco, had been working for over fifteen years on a number of scientifically interesting but publicly obscure basic research projects, funded in part by the government. In 1973, some of his observations led him to collaborate with Dr. Stanley Cohen of Stanford University, who had been working in a complementary field. Together they demonstrated that it was possible to transfer foreign DNA—the basic material that directs life processes—into a microorganism and to have it become part of that organism's genetic structure.

The news of their success was received with great interest throughout the scientific community and elsewhere, but several years would pass before the commercial implications of their work would become widely recognized. When I first contacted Dr. Boyer in early 1976, we were among the very few who then believed that useful products could be developed through this technology in a reasonably short time frame. Within six months of our meeting, we had formed Genentech, developed a business plan, and persuaded a group of venture capitalists to risk their money on our ability to prove two things: that the technology was ready for commercialization, and that we could build a business.

In the following year, 1977, we announced the successful production of the brain hormone somatostatin. This was a significant breakthrough—the first useful protein to be made by recombinant DNA technology. The president of the National Academy of Sciences described the production of somatostatin as a "scientific achievement of the first order."

In the years since then, we have produced many more products by this new technology. In pharmaceuticals, these include human insulin for the treatment of diabetes, human growth hormone for the treatment of growth problems in children, and interferons for antiviral and anticancer indications. In the agricultural area, our first products include bovine and porcine growth hormones. Many other new products are now in various stages of development.

We are proud of what Genentech has accomplished so far. Yet we do not stand alone in illustrating the impact that young, high-technology companies can have on the economy. In 1967, a Commerce Department study found that more than half of all U.S. inventions and innovations were accounted for by small businesses and individual inventors. In 1976, an MIT Development Foundation study found that young technology-oriented companies substantially exceeded their larger, more established competitors in the rates of sales growth, taxes paid, and especially in the number of jobs created. For example, the young technology companies increased jobs at a compound annual rate of 40 percent, compared with less than 1 percent for the mature companies. Other federal studies show that three of every four new jobs created in the private sector in this country can be credited to small business.

The Role of Government

What can the government do to stimulate the formation and growth of new businesses with their subsequent impact on innovation, productivity, and jobs?

Continue to encourage the availability of private funding. Our free enterprise mechanisms for capital formation—especially venture capital—are second to none in the world as a means of supporting the application of science to market needs. Without the necessary funding to develop innovative ideas, many young high-technology companies would not exist today.

Continue to support a strong patent system. Contributions by new business to our national economy are made possible, to a considerable degree, by the protection given to innovation by patents. It would have been difficult for Genentech to have raised the substantial capital needed to fuel our growth and to sustain us during the dry period while our products go through the regulatory approval process, without the potential for protecting our developments. Investor risk would be too great if the products of invention were to become freely accessible too soon to others who have not incurred the same R&D costs. After all, what farmer will invest in seed if the law permits others to take his crops?

Patent protection also makes for a healthier economy by strengthening competition. Under the umbrella of patent, a new company can compete against larger, older, and more entrenched corporations. This, in turn, stimulates the older companies to increase their own R&D efforts, and to lower prices on older products now challenged in the marketplace by new products. I believe that both of those results are desirable from a public policy point of view, in that they provide incentives to continually enrich and extend the nation's research and technology base.

We are encouraged by constructive proposals under consideration in the present session of Congress which, if adopted, will restore the term of a patent that is lost during the regulatory review period. Genentech has testified in favor of patent restoration legislation before House and Senate committees.

Continue to analyze the costs as well as the benefits of regulation.

The impact of regulation often falls heaviest on new businesses, where an infrastructure for handling the paperwork is not yet developed, and where the costs fall mainly on a few newly introduced products. Well before the first sales were made, at least 5 percent of Genentech's employees were dealing primarily with regulatory matters.

Responsible business can and does regulate itself. A good example of the benefits that can flow from a realistic, common-sense, and flexible approach to regulatory issues can be seen in events that took place at the beginning of our industry. In 1976, the National Institutes of Health (NIH) established a Recombinant DNA Advisory Committee (RAC). RAC set up guidelines governing recombinant DNA experiments. Those guidelines were mandatory only for institutions and persons receiving federal funds; but all the companies working in the field, whether federally funded or not, agreed to abide by them. Late in 1982, after reviewing the record carefully, RAC relaxed its requirements, convinced that the safety of this new technology had been well established. No regulations were enacted.

This approach—vigilant and demanding, but flexible and constructive—has enabled recombinant DNA technology to make progress in this country at a rate unparalleled anywhere else in the world. Japan, for example—where regulation of this new technology has been rigid, restrictive—is several years behind the United States in this field.

The Food and Drug Administration (FDA), too, has taken a constructive attitude in making the benefits of biotechnology quickly and safely available to the public. In our own experience, the FDA has eliminated unnecessary studies and has provided us with technical assistance and encouragement as we began the process of taking our first product through the approval system.

In our case, the FDA has been demonstrating that the regulatory burdens can be minimized and that urgently needed drugs can be speeded on their way to those in need, without in any way lowering the agency's high standards for proof of safety and efficacy.

Educational Needs

Thanks to the genius of American scientists, the courage of our venture capitalists, and the cooperative attitude of the NIH and the

183

FDA, the United States now enjoys a significant lead in recombinant DNA technology. But this should not give anyone a feeling of complacency, for that lead is threatened—not by failures in American inventiveness, but by potential shortages in manpower. Highly skilled personnel are vital to this industry. At Genentech, for example, one of every five employees has a Ph.D. degree. Although we are having no difficulty in attracting all the highly qualified men and women we *now* need (thanks in large part to our firm commitment to quality science and peer recognition, including encouraging publication of research papers), government, industry, and the universities will have to act quickly if a bottleneck to growth—such as has been experienced in other high-technology industries—is to be avoided.

Scientifically and technically trained men and women are a critical resource for keeping U.S. industries at the forefront of technological progress. In this area we are clearly falling behind. For example, in 1977—the most recent year for which I have figures—the United States graduated 14,000 electrical engineers, while Japan graduated 19,000. In other words, Japan, with about half the population of our country, graduated nearly 35 percent more electrical engineers than we did. The recent inroads of Japanese companies into the semiconductor industry that our country founded are one result. I am afraid the picture is very similar in other scientific and technical disciplines.

Funding for Basic Research

As a nation, we must encourage our universities to train more scientists and engineers. But it is also important that we provide adequate funding for basic research, that great pool of technical information from which future inventions can be drawn. That funding can and should come from the private sector as well as from the federal government.

There are many ways in which the universities can acquire needed funds through arrangements with business, without impinging on academic freedom. Here too, patents can play a part. For example, Stanford University and the University of California share the basic Boyer-Cohen patent on DNA recombination. I understand that, so far, seventy-one companies (Genentech included) have each agreed to make substantial royalty payments to the universities when they practice under that patent. In other cases, industry grants for graduate training, consulting agreements, and research contracts can supplement government funding of basic research.

Conclusion

This country has a proud history of leadership in transforming scientific discoveries into tangible benefits. Our past successes have resulted in substantial part from sound government policies designed to encourage technological innovation. In this time of unprecedented and competing international and domestic demands, it is imperative that Washington continue a federal policy of stimulating both basic and applied science. In regulating new technologies, utmost caution and restraint should be exercised in order to avoid imposing burdens that might unduly limit the small young companies that characterize high-technology industries. Our lawmakers must keep constantly in mind the needs of innovators, both in the private and the academic sector.

In part, government must provide the incentives. Government must also be alert to root out the disincentives. If government does its part, we can be sure that American business will keep supplying the perspiration and the inspiration that are the common ingredients of innovation.

Determinants of Market Share in
International Semiconductor Markets

M. Thérèse Flaherty

Introduction

Until the mid-1970s, firms based in the United States dominated the world's markets for semiconductor devices and the materials and equipment used in their manufacture. The dominance of U.S. firms seemed to be due primarily to their technological leadership, and not to superior manufacturing or marketing techniques. Recently, however, new foreign entrants have carved out large (in some cases the largest) shares of important semiconductor market segments without having a clear technological advantage. Managers and policymakers in the United States are thus understandably concerned about the relative importance of technological advantage, manufacturing, marketing, and other factors in determining market share.

In this paper I present some observations and hypotheses which may explain how the U.S.-based manufacturers of semiconductor-related products captured their foreign market shares. These conclusions are based on my study (1983) of competition in ten semiconductor product markets which spanned the years from 1960 to 1976. The study was based on personal interviews with technical and

---

The field work for this paper was funded by the Office of Policy Research and Analysis of the National Science Foundation, Grant PRA 7812137. I am indebted to Professor W. Earl Sasser, Jr., for his advice in presenting this material.

professional managers in each company that was a principal in the market segment, as well as published material.

Of course, market shares are not perfect indicators of the profits companies earn. Nor are they perfect indicators of the companies' international competitiveness. However, it seems clear that in the semiconductor industry international competitiveness should be judged with respect to narrowly defined regional product markets. For example, epoxy for integrated circuit encapsulation sold in Western Europe and epoxy sold in the United States differ slightly in formulation and are considered to be in different markets. For such narrowly defined product lines, no profit income statements are available. Market shares are perhaps the best indicators of competitive position in international markets within these market segments.

In this paper I will also focus on the penetration of product markets, to the exclusion of several other aspects of technology competition. Only the products in a functional class which, in retrospect, were successful and had the design that finally became standard in the industry were included in the study. This neglects, of course, the groping, but innovative, efforts of companies competing to achieve the most accepted product. Although this competition, and the costs and incentives which motivate it, are at the core of technological competition, they are all separate from the issue of achieving market penetration after the so-called dominant design has been determined. Some issues related to managing corporate research and development are addressed in Rosenbloom and Kantrow (1981) and Nelson (1981).

I also neglect the advantages and disadvantages in market penetration that might arise in competition between companies based in different countries. For example, if companies based in Japan had a lower cost of capital than those based in the United States, then the Japanese companies might resort to greater capacity or more marketing personnel to penetrate a given foreign market. The retrospective study suggests that base-country advantages affect market share to the extent that external factors in the home country relate to the firm's investments in customer-oriented variables. This paper does not deal with the earlier, preliminary process by which base-country advantages are translated into resources which affect market share in the foreign regional product market. Nor does it take account of any consumer preference for the firms of one country.

187

Government policies to support indigenous firms were surely weaker in Western Europe during the period of the study than in the early 1980s. In Japan there were tariff and nontariff barriers to trade and direct foreign investment; the Japanese manufacturers of digital integrated circuits and the materials and equipment used in their production were weak, relative to the United States, in the competition for state-of-the-art products. To the extent that current host-government policies affect local customer choices, they also mitigate the effects identified here. To the extent that host-government policies are temporary and intended only to give local companies a competitive boost, the earlier Japanese government policies and the more recent policies of Western European governments could be interpreted as subsidies to local companies for building the technological and conventional business resources identified below as being important for market penetration. Judging from the Japanese experience, the consequences of such unilateral protection seem to be competitive advantage and greater market penetration. On the other hand, it is not at all clear that simultaneous countervailing protection—even if all the countries' industries are legitimate candidates for unilateral protection—would benefit companies in any country (Spencer and Brander, 1983).

The Product Technologies Studied

In this study, ten single-product markets listed in Table 1 span the activities of the semiconductor industry. In both the American and foreign regional product markets, all the major competitors were based in the United States. The components examined are: the 4K dynamic RAM (random access memory), an early memory device produced by the high-growth IC manufacturers like Texas Instruments and Intel; the TTL (transistor-transistor logic) family; and the triac, a power control device produced by General Electric Company. Several types of capital equipment and materials produced by companies like Monsanto and Kulicke & Soffa are also examined. These markets are sufficiently developed that they provide an opportunity to study the effects of technology lead, manufacturing decisions, and the marketing mix on market share.

These ten are by no means the only products related to the semiconductor market, but they were representative of the technologies embodied in the components during the 1960s and early 1970s. Experts in each of the three parts of the industry agreed that the products listed included examples of the important component types and the important processes and materials required in the manufacture of components. They were narrowly defined products whose sellers perceived at most four significant direct competitors in any foreign regional market. They were also mature or obsolete products in one of two senses: there are now other products with designs which supersede these and which were widely available, or their total sales were not growing as rapidly as they once had been (in fact, some products were no longer sold).

Product markets in the semiconductor industry do not seem to be defined by the most significant technological discoveries. Fundamental scientific discoveries (like the planar process) were immediately understood and very quickly implemented by all practitioners regardless of firm affiliation. Since the fundamental discoveries were adopted by all competitors so quickly, it seems that companies based their products on proprietary know-how, which is diffused more

TABLE 1 **PRODUCT MARKETS**

Components:	• 4K random access memory
	• Transistor-transistor logic family (TTL)
	• Triac
Equipment:	• Ion implanter
	• Small-Scale Integration/Medium-Scale Integration (SSI/MSI) automatic testing equipment
	• Large-Scale Integration (LSI) automatic testing equipment
	• Molds for plastic encapsulation of integrated circuits
	• Ultrasonic wire bonder
Materials:	• Epoxy for integrated circuit encapsulation
	• Polished single-crystal silicon wafers

slowly. Thus, the speed of diffusion of the proprietary technology embodied in a product may have an important effect on market share. Another critical factor may be the duration of the innovator's technology lead, as discussed below.

The regional markets studied were Western Europe, Southeast Asia (mainly for equipment and materials), and Japan. The products might have been manufactured in the United States and exported; or they might have been components designed and fabricated in the United States, then assembled and tested in Southeast Asia, and finally exported to Western Europe or Japan. What I focus on here is the share of sales—regardless of location of manufacture—of the U.S.-based firms in the regional product market.

Technology Advantage

How would a company's technology advantage affect its share of sales in a foreign market once the product is mature? Is technology itself a competitive tool?

Having a technology lead (in the markets I studied) was not, by itself, an advantage sufficient to ensure capture of a major share of foreign product market. The managers I spoke with universally agreed that having a wholly owned marketing subsidiary was necessary for this. (In Japan, of course, most of the U.S. companies were prohibited from owning marketing subsidiaries. Close relations with local trading companies were the best-available substitute.)

The general notion put forward by the managers I interviewed seems to have been that foreign customers would order directly from the United States only if local marketing was not available. But when local marketing became available, along with an acceptable product, only those companies with a marketing infrastructure were strong competitors. So for new entrants, technology lead alone was not sufficient to gain a lead in foreign sales against a rival with local marketing.

On the other hand, when all firms have a local marketing presence, a technology lead may contribute to market share. The firms in my study that combined a local marketing presence and a technology lead generally had higher market shares than firms with a marketing presence but no technology lead. Interestingly, in one estimation of the full model of market share determination, commercialization of the product accounted, on average, for about 20 of 34 market share points held by technology leaders.

Another possibility, suggested by Schumpeter (1968) in general and by Tilton (1971) in the context of the early history of the semiconductor industry, is that the duration of technology lead can be used to increase profits and market share. Technology lead refers to a period during which the first firm to introduce the product has a monopoly of all customers who decide to buy the new product. Assuming the usual observation to be true that industrial customers are loyal to their original vendor unless problems arise, a longer technological lead should be related to a larger share of customers in the developed market. For technology leaders in this study, however, the relation of market share to the duration of their technology leads was negative.

Some technology leaders developed larger applications engineering efforts than others in the regional product markets. For these companies, market shares were positively related to the duration of their technology leads. This is probably because applications engineers helped customers with their product adoption processes: if few customers adopted the product during the technology lead, then the leader's monopoly was worth very little. For example, the applications engineers employed by one component manufacturer worked directly with the company's customers in designing the component into the customers' products. With the early testing systems for digital logic components, applications engineers developed special programs for each user. Similarly, suppliers of materials frequently worked out different formulations for each client, even though the basic products were very similar. In the early 1970s, for instance, some of the fillers and additives for epoxies differed appreciably from one component manufacturer to another.

Since companies tended to develop their local applications engineering staff slowly for a series of related products, and since significant rivals in the local market usually had an applications engineering presence already when the product was first introduced by the leader, the share of applications engineering effort in the local

191

market was likely to reflect the amount of effort the leader had put into persuading customers to adopt the new product during the technological lead period.

Nontechnological Business Resources

Managers in the semiconductor firms in my study argued that the most important competitive characteristic of their products was their *relative technical quality*. Most firms continually improved their products over the life cycle. Interviewees generally agreed that during the product life cycle their relative positions usually corresponded to the order in which they entered the market. I could find no other indicator of product quality that was comparable across product markets. The possession of a technological lead was, not surprisingly, positively related to higher market shares.

Several important kinds of marketing services that companies provided with their semiconductor products appeared to influence market shares in the product lines. One was *sales effort:* simply visiting customers, and letting them know that the firm would like to make new or repeat sales. Such sales activity seemed to be routine in all three types of semiconductor markets. Sales visits were thought to be necessary, but many managers argued that nothing more substantive need occur than giving the customer this basic attention. An effective local sales effort was positively related to market share in the sample.

Technical service was very important for semiconductor equipment, but not at all important for semiconductor devices and materials. Service people solved routine problems that arose when equipment failed to work as expected in the customer's operation, or needed adjustment during service. For equipment essential for assembly, such as wire bonders and molds used in plastic encapsulation, repairs had to be made quickly, since a plant's entire output could be halted during the shutdown. Technicians flew halfway around the world to adjust or solve this kind of equipment problem. The fragility of the fabrication process for semiconductors, especially for state-of-the-art devices, was also notorious. Humidity and dust can create severe manufacturing problems. Since these problems could halt a component manufacturer's production, customers needed to be able to rely on prompt and efficient service.

Component manufacturers, on the other hand, did not supply service with their products. Components were standardized and inexpensive relative to the cost of troubleshooting individual devices, and were simply replaced when malfunction occurred. This is not to suggest that reliability was unimportant to component users. A particularly alarming malfunction in a component would be handled by an expert applications engineer. Similarly, material suppliers did not have separate technical service staffs, but they offered applications engineering assistance when problems in implementation arose—apparently because such problems with materials usually required considerable expertise.

As expected, equipment manufacturers' market share generally increased with effective local service effort. Interviews also suggested that promptness of delivery was an important consideration for many customers planning to purchase devices, equipment, and materials. Worldwide shortages of semiconductor products, especially devices, had been common since the 1960s. Disruptions of the delicate processes of production inevitably caused delays. Unanticipated surges in demand could also cause shortages. Device manufacturers usually had second sources and secondary production capability in reserve for such situations, but shortages still occurred. In such cases, European and Japanese customers claimed to have had particular difficulty in getting the devices they ordered. They maintained that U.S. customers—whom component manufacturers consider primary—get the devices originally intended for foreign customers. Many also claimed that preferential treatment of U.S. customers was less likely to occur if the firm had a major commitment to the European or Japanese market—for instance, with major investment in local production facilities.

For other reasons, too, a company that set up a local manufacturing facility could be expected to increase its share of local customers. Deliveries from local plants were reputed to be prompt and dependable, and local customers could expect to pay lower prices where no import tariffs are imposed. Moreover, local manufacturing was likely to have larger staffs of applications engineers available, working on high-volume product design or manufacturing, as well as serving customers.

Surprisingly, however, a local manufacturing presence was only weakly related to market shares in the sample of firms studied. It is possible that local manufacturing facilities were established by large companies to satisfy host governments rather than to increase local market share. It is also possible that local manufacturing is primarily a defensive investment: companies might establish local facilities to protect current market share against inroads by competitors (Flaherty and Raubitschek, 1983). Surely the larger issue of what constitutes an effective international manufacturing organization for a market with international competitors goes considerably beyond the individual product market considerations studied here.

Finally, *relative selling price* is usually considered an important determinant of market share. The semiconductor device markets were especially famous for dramatic selling-price reductions over the product life cycle. I have not considered selling price here for two reasons. First, appropriate data were not available. Second, and more important, the managers interviewed and the trade press seemed to agree that price differentials in the equipment and materials markets were not large enough to have an impact on most customers' vendor choice. In device markets, fierce price competition made all the manufacturers' prices decline together, and there was little price dispersion at any one point in time. Some technological leaders in device markets deemphasized the product markets once price had fallen too low; this phenomenon is simply not studied here because it seemed important in so few instances in the sample.

Conclusions and Discussion

From the exploratory field study of ten semiconductor-related products and the U.S.-based companies which sold them in foreign markets, several tentative conclusions can be drawn:

1. Fundamental breakthroughs did not tend to directly generate new products for the companies;
2. The possession of a technological lead without a local marketing infrastructure did not generate market share advantages for the leader;
3. Given a local marketing infrastructure, a technological lead was

necessarily accompanied by a relatively large and effective local applications engineering effort to secure a positive market share;
4. Local sales and service effort was related to larger market share; and
5. A local manufacturing presence had a surprisingly weak relation to market share.

The work supporting these regularities was exploratory. The regularities themselves should be treated as hypotheses rather than as established facts which hold in all markets. In particular, they should not be used in isolation as guides for business or government policy. They could, however, be used in combination with corroborating evidence to guide policies.

Once again, I should note that this study pertains to market share determination, given that a company has introduced an acceptable product. It investigates some effects of international technological competition on market share. But it does not address the determinants of the successful product innovator. The resources and management skills necessary for successful innovation probably differ from those identified here as being necessary for winning a market share; they merit separate study. Such skills are certainly necessary for companies competing in semiconductor-related product markets. Nevertheless, the main way in which American semiconductor companies pay back their investments in innovations is through sales—and thus market share.

REFERENCES

Flaherty, M. T. "Market Share, Technology Leadership, and Competition in International Semiconductor Markets," in R. S. Rosenbloom, ed., *Research on Technological Innovation, Management and Policy*, Vol. 1. Greenwich, Conn.: JAI Press Inc., 1983.

Flaherty, M. T., and Raubitschek, R. S. "Global Resource Deployment in High Technology Competition." Manuscript, 1983.

Nelson, Richard R. "The Role of Knowledge in R&D Efficiency." *Quarterly Journal of Economics*, 97 (1982) : 453–470.

Rosenbloom, Richard S., and Kantrow, Alan M. "The Nurturing of Corporate Research," *Harvard Business Review*, 1982.

Schumpeter, Joseph A. *The Theory of Economic Development.* Cambridge: Harvard University Press, 1968.

Spencer, B. J., and Brander, J. A. "International R&D Rivalry and Industrial Strategy," *The Review of Economic Studies,* 1983.

Tilton, John E. *International Diffusion of Technology: The Case of Semiconductors.* Washington, D.C.: The Brookings Institution, 1971.

U.S. Technological Leadership and Foreign Competition: "De te Fabula Narratur"?

Nathan Rosenberg

THE discussion of America's role in international markets for high-technology products was long dominated by some highly unrealistic expectations. These expectations were formed in the years immediately following World War II, when a whole generation of Americans grew up surrounded by tangible evidence of America's across-the-board technological superiority. For twenty years or so following World War II, and for reasons closely connected with the uneven incidence of that war and its sequelae, American technological leadership was one of the prime facts of international life. The years from 1945 to the middle or late 1960s were, without doubt, an age of American technological hegemony.

Precisely because of their comparative technological backwardness, however, the other OECD member countries were able to combine their recovery not only from wartime destruction, but from a longer period of neglect stretching back to World War I, with a rapid rate of technological improvement. So long as there remained a substantial gap between technology levels in the United States and in the other advanced industrial countries, the possibility existed for rapid rates of technological change through the transfer and adoption of the more sophisticated and productive American technology.

Thus, throughout the 1950s and 1960s, and with varying degrees

A modified version of this paper appeared in Nathan Rosenberg, *Inside the Black Box: Technology and Economics* (New York: Cambridge University Press, 1983).

of effectiveness, the other OECD countries played a highly successful game of technological "catch-up." A combination of high rates of capital formation—on average, far higher than the American—plus the importation and exploitation of more advanced American technologies brought a progressive narrowing of American technological leadership vis-à-vis Europe and Japan.

These developments also expressed themselves in far higher rates of productivity growth abroad by comparison with the United States. This latter trend began to be regarded as alarming in America only in the 1970s when our own rate of productivity growth, which had long been lower than those abroad, fell sharply after a perceptible but slower decline in the late 1960s.

We now find ourselves in a new position. In many fields, America's earlier lonely eminence at numerous technological frontiers has given way to a different situation in which other industrial nations have attained positions close to, or at, these same frontiers. In many ways all this should be cause for rejoicing: we are no longer living in the readily identifiable aftermath of the most destructive war in history. Although we are, perhaps understandably, preoccupied with the more strictly competitive aspects of the situation, we need to be reminded that companionship at the technological frontier offers considerable benefits as well as costs. Indeed, this brings me to one of my central themes. In the years immediately ahead, I would expect to see considerable convergence in the economic environment of a sizable number of countries. In contrast with the postwar years of American hegemony, we are likely to see several technological competitors functioning within increasingly similar economic environments, and therefore responding to increasingly similar stimuli and problems.

It is an entirely plausible notion that the extent of U.S. technological leadership and higher income levels in the early postwar decades limited our capacity to benefit from the technological activities of other countries—at least in terms of transferring useful technology. From this point of view, the growing similarity of conditions in industrial countries is increasing our ability to derive such benefits. More rapidly rising labor costs in Japan and Western Europe and the increasing relative scarcity of certain raw materials in the United States are clearly factors. Foreigners are increasingly responsive to innovative possibilities that will also benefit us, such as labor-saving innovations. Moreover, resource-saving innovations, which have long been of greater use to other countries, are now becoming more relevant and more applicable in the United States. An obvious example is the huge influx of more-energy-efficient Japanese cars. More generally, as real incomes abroad rise more rapidly than in the United States, one may expect a greater number of new products designed mainly for affluent households to enter the U.S. market from abroad.

As a result of these trends, it is already becoming difficult to determine whether certain developments reflect a further erosion of American technological leadership or simply the play of new international market forces. Consider the recent rise in foreign patenting in the United States, a phenomenon that has often been cited as evidence of increasing inventive capability on the part of other countries. It is doubtful that such data really constitute good evidence of the changing relative pace of technological progress. It is more probable that the rising percentage of total U.S. patents taken out by foreigners is a result of commercial judgments respecting such things as changes in the size of specific markets, changes in the composition of demand, changes in relative prices, etc. It is not necessarily evidence of changing technological capabilities.

For instance, some of these changes may reflect the impact of growing concern over environmental pollution and other hazards that have become embodied in government regulations. The rising sensitivity to pollution has considerably increased the proprietary value of high-performance automobile emission control devices and has led to decisions to enter the American market with technologies which, in some cases, had been around for some time. The rise in energy prices may have drastically increased the profitability of energy-conserving technologies in the American market. Because American energy prices have long been below those of the rest of the world, it is reasonable to believe that one result of the rise in energy prices has been to increase considerably the profitability in the U.S. market of energy-saving devices or designs which were *already* in use in other countries. Patents in the U.S. market would thus become more commercially attractive, with no change in relative inventiveness having occurred. Thus, increased patenting by foreigners in the large U.S. market may tell less about changes in relative inventiveness than it does about the changing pattern of incentives that is being generated by underlying economic forces. In some respects, of course, the outcome may be the same, whether the intensifying competitive challenge to an American high-technology firm is the result of shifts in international technological capabilities or of an increasing similarity in the economic conditions of a growing number of industrial countries. From a policy point of view, however, the right diagnosis may make a great deal of difference.

The perspective I have laid out has an additional implication that should be made explicit. The changed American international position is readily subject to a variety of alarmist interpretations. Indeed, I should admit that there are aspects of our recent economic performance that I find particularly alarming, such as the extremely poor productivity growth performance of the American economy during the 1970s. Nevertheless, I believe that policy formulation is not well served by simple extrapolations from the recent past. If I am correct in my analysis of technological "catch-up" abroad and the growing similarity of conditions between the United States and those countries that have been successful in the catch-up process, it would be unwarranted to expect the economic performance of those countries rapidly to surpass that of the United States. On the one hand, rapid technological change becomes much more difficult to sustain as the technological frontier is approached and reached. Catch-up gives way to the more difficult and costly process of jointly pushing out that frontier. Additionally, economies that become affluent will have to share some of the burdens that tend to slow the growth of the technological leader. These include an increasing commitment to improving the quality of the environment; a growing sensitivity to safety and health and other "amenity" considerations; the eventual exhaustion of the pool of labor from low-productivity agricultural occupations that can be applied more productively to other occupations; and the growth of the service sector where, purportedly, productivity improvements are more difficult to attain than in the commodity-producing sector. Thus, an alternative to the scenario in which other industrial countries rapidly surpass America in terms of technological and economic leadership would be one in which a number of countries drift convergently toward some asymptotic level of economic performance, a level first attained by America. As the gaps between them narrow, the "follower" countries increasingly assume certain characteristics of the leader. As Marx, writing of the industrial revolution in England, warned his European readers in the preface to *Capital:* "The country that is more developed industrially only shows, to the less developed, the image of its own future." Or, as he more succinctly put it in the preceding paragraph: "De te fabula narratur!"

A central feature of high-technology industries that is likely to be of increasing significance in the years ahead is an apparently inexorable rise in the development costs of new products. In some measure higher costs are inescapable in a situation where complex, "state-of-the-art" products are being designed and where there are likely to be strong market advantages in performance improvement. Higher performance costs more because there are identifiable tradeoffs of performance versus cost (for example, the use of more costly materials may improve performance). Additionally, the competitive process produces an insistence on bringing the new product into the market ahead of the competition. Greater speed in new product development—in the extreme case, the "crash program" approach—is inherently more costly than a slower, step-by-step, sequential process. This approach is most readily observable in military advanced weapons systems development and in the space program, where cost considerations are accepted as being relatively less important than performance improvement, and where cost overruns are tolerated as an unavoidable fact of life. Although beneficial spillovers from the military and space sectors to the civilian sector are often cited, far less attention has been given to the possibility that such practices may raise the costs of civilian R&D and reduce the sensitivity of American engineers to cost considerations of a kind that are likely to be decisive in commercial markets.

The extreme impact of rising development costs has been particularly apparent in the commercial aircraft industry, especially since the advent of the jet engine in the 1950s. For some years the industry was able to limit development costs by adopting new technologies only after they had been produced and operated for some years in the military. The Boeing 707 was a civilian version of the KC-135 military tanker, an aircraft that had been produced in large numbers for the military; and even the 747 had had the benefit of development experience Boeing derived from its unsuccessful bid in the C5-A competition. With the increased focus upon the missile, however, the military and commercial sectors have diverged. Firms in the commercial sector now face costs of the order of $1 billion to develop a new generation of wide-bodied jets, with less direct financial support from earlier military development projects. Several months ago, McDonnell-Douglas refused an offer by Delta Airlines to undertake the development of a new commercial aircraft, despite Delta's willingness to place an order of over $1.5 billion with the firm.

Thus, commercial aviation firms confront extremely high development costs in addition to the actual costs of production. The situation is compounded by the fact that the market for commercial aircraft is relatively small—partly due to the high productivity and performance of commercial jets. Few commercial jets ever sell more than a couple hundred units—only two (the 727 and the DC-9) have sold in excess of a thousand.

Thus, the extreme commercial risks posed by high development costs are likely to dominate developments in this industry in the future. Subcontracting, as a risk-sharing device in part, is already an important aspect of the industry. For the 747, Boeing had six major subcontractors to share the development costs and risk, and it undertook development of the aircraft only after it had firm purchase commitments in hand from Pan Am, TWA, Lufthansa, and BOAC. Boeing has subcontracting arrangements for its new-generation 767 and 757 with a number of foreign firms—Japanese, Canadian, Italian, and British. It is conceivable that international subcontracting is also motivated by the perception that such arrangements will eventually facilitate commercial entry into those markets.

High development costs and financial risk also figure prominently in the increasing European reliance on international consortia, as in the case of the successful Airbus and the ill-fated Concorde. Although there are now only three commercial airframe manufacturers and two commercial jet engine manufacturers in the United States, the numbers are even smaller in Western Europe, where the industry is largely nationalized. In addition, it is important to note that the Concorde, a brilliant engineering achievement but a commercial disaster (only sixteen were manufactured before production was discontinued), was made possible by immense subsidies from the French and British governments.

Increasing development costs and financial risks are also apparent in other high-technology industries. There are obvious parallels throughout the field of military procurement—with the additional special problem of a single buyer. Development costs of nuclear power reactors, where safety and environmental considerations are especially important, have moved inexorably upward. Conventional power-generating equipment, although not plagued by the special problems of nuclear power, also presents technological and other performance problems that have resulted in very high development costs. The exploitation of new fossil fuel energy sources, involving liquefaction and gasification, is almost certain to encounter spectacular development costs, as is already abundantly apparent at the pilot-plant stage. Telecommunications, involving unique problems of systemic complexity, compatibility, and interdependence and the special features associated with network evolution, also encounters very high development costs (the cost of the #4 Electronic Switching System was around $400 million). Finally, although the electronics industry has very different features from the industries just mentioned, the design and development of reliable, high-capacity memory chips has drastically raised the table stakes for commercial survival. Almost daily, reports in the financial press suggest that hundreds of millions of dollars in development costs are being incurred in the international competition for the 64K RAM market. Prospects for recovering these development costs are jeopardized by widespread price cutting.

Thus, industries confronting a combination of a dynamic, rapidly improving technology and high levels of development costs share, in varying degrees, a range of common problems. Financial risks sometimes necessitate markets substantially larger than can be provided by a single moderate-sized Western European country. For technological and other reasons (sometimes regulatory), long lead times are often involved that (at best) defer the full recovery of financial outlays into the distant future. Not only are uncertainties over technological factors particularly great, but the largest financial commitments are often required during the early stage, when uncertainties are greatest. Rapid technological change also raises the risk of investing in long-lived plant and equipment, since further change is likely to render such capital obsolete. If, as is widely asserted, product life cycles are themselves becoming shorter, the risk is further increased. What is certainly true is that the question of timing in the commitment of large amounts of resources to the development process becomes even more crucial. There is abundant evidence in recent history that new, technologically complex products experience numerous difficulties in their early stages that may take years to iron out. The earliest Schumpeterian innovators frequently wind up in the bankruptcy courts. The strategy of a rapid imitator, or "fast second," benefiting from the mistakes of the pioneer, has much to commend it, especially when rapid technological change is expected to continue. This was clearly the case with British pioneering of the commercial Comet I, well before American entry into the commercial jet age. As it happened, substantial improvements in engine performance in the next couple of years offered Boeing and Douglas decisive commercial advantages, in terms of greater capacity and speed, that were incorporated into their later entrants, the 707 and DC-8.

The development process eventually dovetails into investment in plant and equipment. Indeed, in a high-technology world of prototypes and pilot plants it may be impossible to draw a sharp line of demarcation between the two. There are even more ways in which high-technology industries are bringing the two stages closer together. It is increasingly characteristic of some of these industries that the performance of the final product as well as the efficiency of the production process are extremely sensitive to the nature of the manufacturing process technology. In electronics, yield and performance rely on the maintenance of scrupulously high standards of cleanliness and other aspects of quality control. Thus, innovation in electronics has created a greater degree of intimacy between product and process innovation, both of which now need to be considered together. The great increase in circuit-element density, leading to dramatic improvements in the capabilities of an integrated circuit chip, has been inseparable from the introduction of more complex processing equipment. This processing equipment, in turn, raised the fixed costs of a wafer fabrication plant from $2 million to $50 million during the 1970s. Such plants, of course, need to operate at very large volumes.

Here again, the thrust of high-technology innovation is to require greater output and to push producers beyond the limited domestic markets. For a variety of reasons, including tariffs and other forms of protective legislation that place imported products at a competitive disadvantage, multinational firms may attempt to exploit specific foreign markets by establishing a local subsidiary. Such actions obviously accelerate the transfer of technology; indeed, multinational firms are now a main instrument for the more rapid international diffusion of advanced technologies. (Other factors are the improved technologies of transportation and communication as well as the increasing numbers of students studying abroad.)

In an increasingly interdependent world, it becomes more and more difficult to isolate the domestic and international contexts of decisions relating to the innovative process. Therefore, it is not enough to argue that efforts to transfer a technology overseas will narrow the technology gap between the United States and the rest of the world. Obviously in making the initial decision to undertake the development of a new technology, a high-technology firm will take into account the prospect of earning revenues from innovation overseas as well as in domestic markets. How substantial these prospects may be is a difficult matter of commercial judgment, but it seems apparent that the willingness of American firms to undertake development expenditures at home is increased by the possibility of eventually transferring the technology overseas in some manner. To the extent that such a factor is at work, the ability to do so will strengthen the willingness of companies to commit resources to the innovation process. The shorter product life cycles and more rapid diffusion of new technologies discussed earlier mean that the prospect of such overseas payoffs is an important incentive. And yet there are drawbacks even here. A speeding up of the international diffusion of new technologies would seem to assure a shorter time period in which an innovating firm can exploit its technological lead.

An increasingly interdependent world with rapidly advancing technologies also calls into serious question the view of an "industry" as a distinct, indivisible unit. A case in point is the ongoing dissolution of the boundary line between the telecommunications and computer industries. The microchip revolution and the growing information-processing needs of business are converting computers into forms that increasingly resemble telecommunications networks, while the telephone system has already become, in a very real sense, a gigantic computer. More generally, reduced transportation costs—or the increasing prominence of industries where transportation costs are relatively insignificant, such as electronics—make possible new divisions of labor. Such arrangements make it feasible for an industry to parcel out separate activities or components on a truly international basis. Thus, buyers of Boeing's forthcoming 767 will purchase an airframe the components of which have been manufactured in several countries on different continents. Boeing will happily deliver the aircraft equipped with American engines (Pratt and Whitney or General Electric) or British engines (Rolls-Royce) to suit the preferences of the buyer. The European Airbus, on the other hand, comes equipped with American engines (General Electric).

The present situation in the computer industry is one of continued American dominance of world markets (about 80 percent of the total), but with such growing Japanese domination in memory chips that there is fear of an eventual Japanese monopoly of that strategic component. A situation in which the United States dominates the brains of the computer—the logic circuits—while the Japanese dominate the memory circuits is perfectly conceivable. Additionally, although there is an increasing use of Japanese components, American manufacturers continue to dominate the mainframe market. Finally, although Japanese performance in hardware continues to improve, American superiority in software remains overwhelming. The American dominance of software accounts, in turn, for the inability of the Japanese to make larger inroads into the rapidly expanding minicomputer and personal computer markets, where software is especially crucial.

The purpose of these examples is emphatically *not* to suggest that the areas of American and Japanese strength will continue to be demarcated along present lines. That would be foolhardy. Rather, it is to suggest the possibility of entirely new patterns of specialization at the common technological frontier, as the participants at that frontier become more numerous. These new patterns may well be such that it makes little sense to apply terms such as "technological leadership" or "technological gaps" to entire industries, much less entire countries. There may be reasons for a country to persistently retain technical and commercial superiority in specific segments of an industry which do not allow it to dominate the entire industry.

We should also recognize the limits of the technological variable itself to explain performance and position. Success in high-technology markets is not reducible to mere technological capability. Such success is also a matter of organizational flexibility, managerial effectiveness, the social and economic rewards of risk-taking, the efficiency of capital markets, and a number of other "environmental" factors that may affect the ability to convert technological opportunities into commercially successful innovations, whether these opportunities first emerge at home or abroad.

Finally, there is a series of questions that need to be addressed concerning the interface between science and technology—and it is perhaps the intensity of activity at that interface that really defines a high-technology industry in the first place. The long-term vitality of such industries is directly dependent upon the degree of success in achieving creative interactions between the two realms. Yet we are far from having a good understanding of the conditions that make for successful interactions, and how such conditions can be encouraged.

To begin with, there remain crucial segments of high-technology industries where attempts to advance the state of the art are painstakingly slow and expensive because of the limited guidance available from science. The development of new alloys with specific combinations of properties proceeds very slowly because there is still no adequate theoretical basis for predicting the behavior of new combinations of materials. Many problems connected with improved fuel efficiency are severely constrained by the limited scientific understanding of the combustion process. The development of synthetic fuels is at present seriously hampered by our scientific ignorance with respect to the molecular structure of coal and the relationship of that structure to its chemical properties. The design of aircraft and steam turbines is hampered by the lack of a good theory of turbulence. In the case of aircraft, wind tunnel tests are still subject to substantial margins of error in terms of predicting actual flight performance. Indeed, to a considerable extent the high development costs with which this paper is concerned are due precisely to the inability to draw more heavily upon a predictive science in determining the performance of new designs or materials. If science provided a better predictive basis for moving to optimal design configurations, development costs (which constitute about two-thirds of total R&D expenditures in the United States) would not be nearly so high.

On the other hand, scientific progress itself has become increasingly dependent upon the realm of technology. Much scientific progress, in advanced industrial societies, derives from the attempt to account for anomalous or unexpected observations or difficulties that arise in connection with the productive process. In addition, technological progress in the design and construction of scientific instruments has enormously expanded the observational capabilities of science. Our understanding of the complex molecular structure of polymers, for example, would be far less advanced if not for an array of twentieth-century scientific instruments—X-ray diffraction equipment, the ultracentrifuge, the electron microscope, the viscometer, etc. To an increasing degree, the linkage between science and technology is proving to be a powerful stimulus to science, which in turn feeds back into the productive process.

A central concern for the formulation of policy ought to be how to improve the organizational conditions and incentive structure at the science-technology interface. The ability to improve the functioning of that interface will undoubtedly be an important determinant of future leadership in high-technology industries. This is so not only for the reasons already indicated, but also because changes appear to be occurring on the side of science as well as technology. For example, there is evidence that scientific knowledge of the kind more likely to be useful to high-technology industries has to be pursued in an increasingly interdisciplinary fashion. The transistor was the work of physicists, chemists, and metallurgists. The scientific breakthrough leading to the discovery of DNA was the work of chemists, biologists, biochemists, and crystallographers. Historically, new disciplines such as biochemistry have emerged when practitioners of separate disciplines—e.g., biology and chemistry—discovered an interesting range of problems at the boundaries of their respective disciplines. Unfortunately, such interdisciplinary research frequently runs counter to the organizational arrangements, priorities, and incentive structures of the scientific professions—although this is admittedly more true in the academic world than in the industrial world. Nevertheless, there may be a high social payoff in enabling at least some larger subgroup of the scientific community to define its activities in terms of problem orientation rather than of discipline orientation. This will make it easier to undertake joint research of an interdisciplinary nature when such directions appear to be promising.

The most successful research institutions in private industry have already demonstrated that it is possible to conduct research of both a fundamental and an interdisciplinary nature in a commercial, "mission-oriented" context. In addition, the United States has shown itself to be capable of a high degree of institutional creativity by inventing public-sector mechanisms for the performance of research in specific fields. The land grant colleges and agricultural experiment stations have played important roles in exploiting the regionally diverse agricultural resources of the country; the National Institutes of Health have played a vital part in advancing the frontiers of medical research; and the National Advisory Committee on Aeronautics (the predecessor of NASA) played a critical role in generating empirical data for the design of new aircraft that made an essential contribution to American worldwide leadership in the commercial aircraft industry. Devising new ways of encouraging a closer and more creative interaction at the science-technology interface would thus seem to be both feasible and in line with our own pragmatic traditions.

Biographies of Authors

M. THERESE FLAHERTY is Assistant Professor at the Harvard Business School. Her research and teaching there focus on the management of international production and technology. She has conducted a field study, on which the paper that appears here is based, of international technology transfer by U.S.-based semiconductor companies. She has also contributed to the modeling literature in the economics of dynamic competition.

Before Harvard, she taught economics at Stanford University. She received her Ph.D. in economics from Carnegie-Mellon University in 1976 and her B.S. in mathematics and economics from Tufts University in 1972. She spent a year studying at the London School of Economics.

RALPH E. GOMORY is Vice President and Director of Research for the IBM Corporation. He is responsible for IBM's research laboratories in Yorktown Heights, N.Y.; San Jose, Calif.; and Zurich, Switzerland. Dr. Gomory joined IBM in 1959 as a research mathematician at Yorktown Heights. In 1964 he was made an IBM Fellow, a rank conferred on a small number of scientists and engineers by IBM. In 1970 he was named Director of Research and was elected a Vice President in 1973. Dr. Gomory is a member of the National Academy of Sciences and National Academy of Engineering. He is a Chairman of the Advisory Council of the Department of Mathematics, Princeton University, and a member of the Advisory Council, School of Engineering, Stanford University.

CARL KAYSEN is the David W. Skinner Professor of Political Economy and Director of the Program in Science, Technology, & Society at the Massachusetts Institute of Technology. He received his Ph.D. in economics in 1954 and was a member of the Harvard Economics Department from 1950 to 1966. Dr. Kaysen served as Deputy Assistant to President Kennedy for National Security from 1961 to 1963. Before joining the faculty at MIT, he was Director of the Institute for Advanced Study (1966–1976) and was also the Vice Chairman and Director of Research for the Sloan Commission on Government and Higher Education from 1977 to 1979.

HAROLD PAUL LUKS is Staff Consultant to the Subcommittee on International Economic Policy and Trade, Committee on Foreign Affairs, U.S. House of Representatives. Previously he was Director of International Trade Consulting Services, Executive Director of a private commission on international economic policy chaired by Paul McCracken and Henry Fowler, and Senior Legislative Assistant to Senator Abraham A. Ribicoff. He is a graduate of Pennsylvania State University and has pursued doctoral studies at George Washington University.

RICHARD R. NELSON is Professor of Economics and Director, Institution for Social and Policy Studies, Yale University. Prior to joining the faculty at Yale he was an economist for the Rand Corporation and a senior staff member of the Council of Economic Advisers.

Dr. Nelson received his B.A. degree from Oberlin College and his Ph.D. from Yale University. In addition to teaching at Yale, he has taught at Oberlin College and the Carnegie Institute of Technology.

Dr. Nelson's research has primarily concerned the processes of long-run economic change, with particular emphasis on technological advance and on the evolution of economic institutions.

WILLIAM NORDHAUS is John Musser Professor of Economics at Yale University and a staff member of the Cowles Foundation for Research in Economics. He served from 1977 to 1979 as a member of the Council of Economic Advisers under President Carter and is the author of several books, including *Reforming Federal Regulation, The Efficient Use of Energy Resources,* and *Invention, Growth, and Welfare.*

WILLIAM J. PERRY is an Executive Vice President of Hambrecht & Quist Incorporated, an investment banking firm in San Francisco specializing in high-technology companies. Prior to joining H&Q, he was Under Secretary of Defense for Research & Engineering. As the Under Secretary, he was responsible for all weapon systems procurement and all research and development; he was the Secretary of Defense's principal advisor on technology, communications, intelligence, and atomic energy.

Dr. Perry received his B.S. and M.S. from Stanford University and his Ph.D. from Penn State, all in mathematics. He has been a lecturer in mathematics at Santa Clara University and currently is a Senior Fellow at Stanford University. He was elected to the National Academy of Engineering in 1970.

NATHAN ROSENBERG is currently Professor of Economics and Department Chairman at Stanford University. He has taught economics at Indiana, Pennsylvania, Purdue, Harvard, and Wisconsin and has lectured extensively in Europe, Asia, and South America. His long-standing interest in economic growth and the role played by technological change in generating that growth has taken him into economic history, a field where he has also written extensively. In addition, Rosenberg has served on numerous governmental committees dealing with issues related to technological change. His most recent book is *Inside the Black Box: Technology and Economics,* published by Cambridge University Press.

ROBERT A. SWANSON was 28 years old when he and Dr. Herbert Boyer founded Genentech, Inc., in 1976. Prior to that time, Mr. Swanson was a partner with Kleiner & Perkins venture capital partnership, and from 1970 to 1974 he was an investment officer with Citicorp Venture Capital Ltd. Mr. Swanson has a B.S. degree in chemistry from Massachusetts Institute of Technology and an M.S. degree from the Alfred P. Sloan School of Management at MIT.

Index

advanced technology, 24–31
  core technologies and, 29–30
  definition of, 24–25
  diffused throughout economy, 29–30
  as national priority, 6, 14, 15, 18, 24, 26–31, 55–56, 57
  national security reliant on, 7, 26
advanced technology industries, 148
  all-or-nothing vs. incremental decision-making in, 74, 77
  capital for, 177–78, 179
  classification of, 22n
  dissolution of industry boundaries in, 205–6
  economic well-being and, 20, 26
  fostering new businesses in, 182–83
  impact of young companies in, 181
  large markets needed by, 74, 203, 204–5
  new ventures in, European vs. U.S., 169
  pace of technological change in, 73–74, 77
  product and process innovation linked in, 204
  reciprocity legislation and, 148, 150
  rising development costs in, 201–4
  role of management in, 10–11, 15, 16, 57, 58
  science-technology interface and, 207–9
  success factors in, 206–7
  see also biotechnology; computer industry; microelectronics industry; telecommunications
advanced technology trade, 11–13, 18–21, 36–42
  cooperation among industrial groups in, 41
  depressed world economy and, 11–12, 19–20
  disputes over acceptable practices in, 11, 12–13, 15, 19, 57
  dollar valuation and, 20, 21, 76

  domestic suppliers favored in, 37, 38, 39
  emerging Third World market and, 36
  export credits in, 35, 38, 40, 47, 143, 145, 157–58
  foreign investment restrictions and, 37, 39
  foreign subsidiaries in, 37, 39
  frictions among industrialized allies and, 18–19, 38
  as high priority, 18
  inequalities of government backing in, 11, 15, 19, 44, 53, 57
  market fragmentation in, 35, 37–38
  market share determinants in, 186–195
  market sharing or technical cooperation in, 40
  most deleterious practices in, 38–41
  negotiations needed in, 12–13, 16–17, 38–42, 58–59
  nontariff barriers in, 36–37, 39
  predatory pricing in, 39
  pressures on third-country markets in, 39–40
  subsidy policies in, 40, 42n
  targeting of U.S. markets in, 39
  trade balance in, 27–29
  U.S. market share of, 20–21, 29
  U.S. objectives in, 12, 16–17
  see also trade policy, U.S.
agriculture, 29, 200, 209
Airbus Industrie, 21, 23n, 202, 206
aircraft industry, 21, 23n, 96, 99, 108, 201–2, 204, 205–6, 207, 209
Air Force, U.S., 27
American Electronics Association, 177
antidumping statutes, 123, 125, 134
antitrust policies, 41, 78, 121, 158, 164
  domestic competition and, 46
  international competitiveness and, 45–46, 145, 157
  research consortia and, 40

215